Singers' Italian

A Manual of Diction and Phonetics

by Evelina Colorni

Faculty, Juilliard School •

Diction Coach, San Francisco Opera Merola Program

SCHIRMER BOOKS

A Division of Macmillan Publishing Co., Inc.

NEW YORK

COLLIER MACMILLAN PUBLISHERS

LONDON

SCHIRMER BOOKS
A Division of Macmillan Publishing Co., Inc.
866 Third Avenue, New York, N.Y. 10022

Collier Macmillan Canada, Ltd.

Library of Congress Catalog Card Number: 71-113927

Printed in the United States of America

printing number
3 4 5 6 7 8 9 10

ISBN : 0–911320–03–2

PREFACE

This book is meant primarily for singers, but it may be of equal interest to those who concern themselves with singing—voice teachers, coaches, accompanists, choral and orchestral conductors, editors and composers. It deals with Italian phonetics as used in lyric diction and considers the changes that occur between the manner in which a language is spoken and the way in which it is sung. These changes are due to the inherent differences between speech and song. Since it is written for the singer whose native language is English and who wishes to sing Italian, it is based on a constant comparison between Italian and English.

Through the centuries, Italian has played a very special role in the training of voices, a role directly linked with a particularly fortunate pattern of speech sounds which is conducive to singing, and to releasing the voice. To achieve such a release, and to obtain the best vocal results, it is imperative that the pattern of Italian speech sounds, and the norms governing them in words and phrases, be understood and adhered to. Unless they are, it is senseless to train young vocalists to sing arias from the Italian repertoire. Only too frequently students are allowed to sing Italian while using native English speech sounds.

English-speaking singers tend to believe that Italian is easy to sing. Compared to French and German, Italian may seem easy but this is deceptive, for the phonetic principles underlying Italian are often diametrically opposed to those of English. To master them, concentrated study and practice are required.

This book is planned to guide the singer, by means of discussion and drill, toward the acquisition of an efficient and effective Italian diction. This in turn should lead him to increased physiological freedom and vocal growth.

The Italian which is considered standard, and advocated here, is the cultured language spoken in Florence, the Florentine devoid of regionalisms. It is the language spoken by the best actors of the legitimate stage.

The alphabet of the International Phonetic Association has been chosen as the most satisfactory and widely used means of conveying speech sounds.

When used as a classroom text book, Parts I to IV should be the core of the first year's work, supplemented by whatever basic introduction to Part VII the instructor deems necessary. A good way to start would be to alternate vowel drill with drill of the dental consonants.

To increase its practical value as a reference book, numerous subsections have been adopted to classify its contents.

Among the many persons to whom I owe so much in my professional life, I would like to mention the late Nicola Zingarelli, Professor of Neolatin Languages at the University of Milan, who more than anyone awakened my understanding of language; and Maestro Arturo Toscanini who first introduced me to the world of opera, to his world of opera, and later invited me to coach diction to singers who performed in the N.B.C.'s opera productions under his baton. To watch and follow him in his work taught me more than I will ever be able to acknowledge. He used to say to his singers: "Say the word, and the tone will come by itself." To him one great challenge in vocal performance was diction, which might be another clue to his unique artistry.

I am deeply indebted to Mr. Otto Guth, New York operatic coach and Musical Supervisor of the San Francisco Opera, and to Miss Marion Schild of the Library of Congress for reading my typescript and giving most valuable suggestions.

Finally, I would like to acknowledge that this book would not have been written without the kind encouragement of Mr. William Schuman. He suggested that I expand a brochure on Italian Lyric Diction, which I had written, into a book. SINGERS' ITALIAN is the result.

CONTENTS

PART III

THE CONSONANTS

PART IV

THE SEMICONSONANTS

INTRODUCTION

1 WHAT IS LYRIC DICTION?

There is a difference between studying a foreign language and learning to sing in it. To master a foreign language one has to be able to speak and understand it and to read and write it as well. Its study involves the development of skill and comprehension and requires a knowledge of vocabulary, grammar, syntax, pronunciation and intonation. To learn a foreign language so as to master it like one's own is a long and slow process.

To learn to sing in a foreign language is a simpler task. It is, of course, advisable for the singer to have a reading knowledge of the language so that he may have a thorough understanding of the text. An acquaintance with the fundamentals of the language, and the ability to use a grammar and dictionary, should fulfill this need.

What the singer will have to concentrate upon most is the delivery of the song, for which diction ranks as high as voice. Human as some instruments such as a cello or a French horn may sound, it is only when man sings that a tune and an articulate message are combined.

What is lyric diction? According to Webster, it is the rendition of words in singing with regard to pronunciation, enunciation and expression.

Pronunciation deals with the proper choice of speech sounds and enunciation with the accuracy with which these sounds should be uttered. Expression is the act of conveying the full meaning of every phrase, song or aria.

A singer's art depends heavily on his power of expression, and for this very reason he should first dedicate himself to the study of pronunciation and enunciation. Only through their mastery will he be able to express his feelings as he desires.

Pronunciation and enunciation are interdependent and in dealing with the one it will often be necessary to touch upon the other. But it is with the study of pronunciation that this book will begin.

2 A GENERAL DISCUSSION OF PRONUNCIATION AND PHONETICS

Pronunciation is that aspect of diction which deals with the correct choice of speech sounds. If anybody says *zis* for *this,* he is using a wrong speech sound and is mispronouncing this word.

Children learn to speak through imitation. Likewise, adults learning a foreign language will often resort to imitation in a trial and error fashion. However, a more accurate and quicker way to learn pronunciation is through the scientific study of the speech sounds and their formation. This science is called "Phonetics."

A spoken language may be considered as a sequence of speech sounds. Some basic differences among spoken languages arise from the various speech sounds peculiar to each language. For example, among the Western languages of primary interest to a Western singer, only English has *th* sounds as in *thumb* and *then;* only French has nasal vowels, as in *chant, pin, nom, brun;* and only German has *ch* sounds as in *ich* and *ach*.

If we consider how conventional English spelling relates to pronunciation, we find many inconsistencies. Often a letter represents different sounds, as the letter *s* in *sore, sure, rose, pleasure*. Also, the same sound may be spelled in different ways, as the sound *ee* in *see, sea, he, key, quay, piece*. There are instances when letters are silent, as the *k* in *knave,* or the *g* in *gnat*. Furthermore, two letters may stand for a single sound, as the *th* in *thaw,* and the *ph* in *phrase*. And, conversely, a single letter may represent two sounds, as the *y* in *my* and the *u* in *mule*.

Such discrepancies between conventional English spelling and pronunciation make it impossible to determine the pronunciation from the spelling. Similar inconsistencies exist in all languages. For this reason linguistic scholars felt the need for a new and different alphabet, one which would indicate the exact pronunciation of all languages, regardless of their spelling. Around 1888 the International Phonetic Association was founded to devise such a pronouncing alphabet. It is known as the "International Phonetic Alphabet" (IPA).

To the conventional letters, new ones were added to make this alphabet serve its phonetic purpose. Each letter of the IPA symbolizes one sound only, always the same one, regardless of the language in which the sound occurs, and regardless of how it is conventionally spelled. The IPA symbols are named by the sound each represents. They are enclosed in brackets so as to distinguish them from the letters of the Roman alphabet used in conventional spelling.

Because of its nature, the IPA facilitates the task of identifying speech sounds and isolating them for the purpose of study and comparison. Being a key to all languages, it is the perfect tool for a singer. The more accurately he realizes which sounds languages have in common, and which sounds they do not, the better will he be able to grasp the sound pattern peculiar to each language.

The student should know that, unlike English, which is essentially unphonetic, Italian is highly phonetic. This means that its spelling is mostly related to sound. In the few instances where it is not, the IPA will be of great help in clarifying the issues.

3 CLASSIFICATION OF SPEECH SOUNDS

Speech sounds are generally classified as vowels and consonants.

Vowels may be roughly defined as continuous voiced speech sounds produced without constriction or obstruction in the pharynx and mouth.

Conversely, consonants are speech sounds characterized by a constriction or stoppage of the flow of breath by the organs of speech.

In addition, there is a third category partaking of the nature of both vowels and consonants and appropriately called semiconsonants and semivowels.

All three types of sounds appear in Italian.

4 ENGLISH VOWELS

A brief discussion of English vowels may further clarify the phonetic approach.

English, which in conventional spelling uses the Roman alphabet, has five vowel letters, *a, e, i, o* and *u*. But if one listens with a trained ear to spoken English, one is able to hear not five but approximately fifteen vowel sounds. Here the accuracy of the IPA is helpful, for it has a symbol for each of these fifteen sounds.

Every vowel is the result of a particular position of the tongue and lips and phoneticians have found it pertinent to classify vowel sounds according to the position of the tongue. Accordingly, spoken English is said to have six front, six back and three mid vowels.

The six front vowels, so called because they are spoken with the tongue fronted (see Part I, Section 1(A)), are [i] as in *see,* [ɪ] as in *fit,* [e] the first vowel of *chaotic,* [ɛ] as in *well,* [æ] as in *had* and [a] as in *dance.*

The six back vowels, so called because they are spoken with the tongue backed (see Part I, Section 1(B)), are [u] as in *who,* [ʊ] as in look, [o] first vowel of *omit,* [ɔ] as in *jaw,* [ɒ] as in *gone* and [ɑ] as in *calm.*

The three mid vowels, so called because they are spoken with the middle of the tongue slightly raised are [ɜ] as in *sir,* [ə] the final vowel of *never* and [ʌ] as in *blood.*

Phoneticians have developed a chart of the vowel sounds of each language and have arranged each category of vowels in such a way that they form a progressive sequence. To offer the singer a chance for comparison with the chart of Italian vowels (see Part I, Section 1), here is how a phonetic chart of the vowels of spoken English may look:

Front Vowels		*Mid Vowels*		*Back Vowels*	
bee	i			u	boom
bit	ɪ			ʊ	book
ch*a*otic	e			o	*o*bey
bet	ɛ	ɜ	burn	ɔ	ball
bat	æ	ə	the	ɒ	bomb
bass	a	ʌ	bud	ɑ	balm

Speak the front vowels from top to bottom and watch in a mirror how the tongue, lip and jaw positions change. Do the same with the back and mid vowels.

5 FRENCH, GERMAN AND ITALIAN VOWELS

Like the English, the French, Germans and Italians use the Roman alphabet. Therefore they have the same five vowel letters, *a, e, i, o* and *u*. But these letters represent a different number of vowel sounds in each language.

In English, there are fifteen "front," "back" and "mid" vowels; in French, sixteen "front," "back," "mixed" and "nasal" vowels; in German, fourteen "front," "back" and "mixed" vowels. In Italian, however, there are only seven. These are "front" and "back" vowels only.

Such front and back vowels, common to all four languages, are called basic or fundamental vowels.

6 HOW TO PRACTICE

As with any other skill, practice is essential in learning the diction of a language. In Part I, Section 3, for instance, each vowel sound will be described according to its distinctive acoustic characteristics and the required position of the speech organs involved. Such description will be followed by practice material drawn from the standard operatic repertoire.

One should concentrate first upon learning how to produce each vowel in isolation. When it can be said accurately and with ease, one should proceed to practice syllables, words and phrases containing the sound.

Exercises should be spoken before they are sung. Only when the movements required by the speech organs have become easy and automatic should one proceed to singing the exercise.

Vowels, syllables and single words may be sung on any comfortable pitch or scale. If the operatic phrases are unfamiliar, or do not lie in one's voice range, one may sing them on a monotone, or on any notes that feel comfortable.

BODY ALIGNMENT

When practicing, careful thought should be given to body alignment. The jaw will drop easily and the tongue function efficiently if the head and spine are well aligned.

A singer must build his body into an efficient instrument that will serve him well. In an article titled REQUISITE FOR AUDIBILITY, published in the drama section of the New York Times on March 24, 1957, Paul Heinberg (then professor of speech at Oklahoma State University) answers his own question "Why posture exercises?" with the following: "The spine provides the base upon which the cords operate, and this base must be substantial if they are to function well." This base must be just as substantial if the speech organs are to function well.

The best way to sit is with both feet flat on the floor and the knees straight. The suggestion to sit and stand tall has often proved helpful.

TONGUE EXERCISES

One should practice with a mirror. This will allow for an objective visual control of the speech organs, and is more reliable than vague subjective feelings.

For the beginner, the control of the tongue, lips and jaw is a valuable aid for attaining correct sounds. Later, after sufficient practice, it will be easy to evoke and utter them without much thought of muscular adjustment. But at the beginning, the singer should conscientiously follow all instructions.

With all seven Italian vowel sounds the tip of the tongue should be in contact with the lower front teeth. This is achieved not through muscular effort of the tongue itself but as the natural result of a relaxed, and therefore extended, tongue. When the tongue is so relaxed that the tip stays in easy contact with the lower teeth, the front or back of the tongue will be able to adjust to the required position with ease and efficiency. Also, the throat will remain open, since it is not crowded by the bulk of a tense tongue. This is of no mean advantage to a singer.

An essential prerequisite for a correct vowel production is a loose tongue devoid of tension. And since it is the vowels which carry the tone, the voice will profit from a relaxed tongue. This is the reason why many books on speech or diction have special sets of tongue exercises.

At this point, we are not going to list any special tongue exercises. We will simply refer to Part III, Section 3, on the Dental Consonants and urge the singer not to rush through these exercises. For in addition to training him in the correct dentalization of *l, n, d, t* and *r,* they will give the tongue looseness, flexibility and agility.

TRAINING THE EAR

In the process of learning to speak a new language or in perfecting one's own, ear training plays a prominent role since one cannot produce a speech sound unless one is first able to "think" the sound correctly—that is, to hear it within oneself.

A sound is learned by hearing it. One listens to it attentively, actively, repeatedly until it is grasped by the ear and intellect and can be reproduced accurately.

Ear training is as essential in language as in music and the ideal way to learn pronunciation is through drill under the guidance of a phonetically trained teacher.

But, there is another method of conveying the characteristics of a speech sound—through the minute description of the required position and movements of the speech organs—tongue, lips, teeth, palate, jaw, etc.

This book will endeavor to do this, as well as to compare the acoustic qualities of an Italian sound with the related English sound; or, if indicated, with the French or German one.

If a singer works alone, the responsibility for his ear training rests with himself. To achieve results he will have to enunciate his practice material audibly, forcefully and distinctly, and to learn how to listen to himself. Only then will he be able to develop the necessary auditory control which will allow him to bring out his linguistic and artistic potentials.

Listening actively and critically to instructors, singers and actors also plays an important role in deepening one's aural sensibilities. Still, for a singer, whose art requires excellent diction, the mere thinking of sounds (silent practice) or mumbling or whispering them will lead nowhere. He will have to learn to use a strong, well-supported voice. Gradually he will come to realize the analogy between speaking a text slowly and accurately, with a well-supported voice, and singing it.

This seems the place to mention the English speech sounds which this book will use for comparison.

People speak their mother tongue in many different ways. The English of an American differs from that of a Briton, Canadian or Australian. Also, a New Englander speaks differently from a Southerner or a Midwesterner.

Actually, no two persons speak a sound in an identical way. For the speech organs depend on the build of one's body, particularly the skull. In spite of these variations there still remains the possibility of comparing, for example, the main characteristics of an Italian [i] with the main characteristics of the English [i].

Since it cannot be taken for granted that all readers have been trained in English lyric diction, the English sounds used here for comparison will be those which are considered standard in accepted, good American speech devoid of regional accents.

Chart I

CHART OF ITALIAN SOUNDS

CONSONANTS:		Bilabials		Labiodentals		Dentals		Prepalatals		Mediopalatals	
	Plosives	p	b			t	d			k	g
Continuants	Nasals		m				n		ɲ		ŋ
	Laterals						l		ʎ		
	Vibrants						ɾ r				
	Fricatives			f	v	s	z	ʃ			
	Affricates					ts	dz	tʃ	dʒ		
SEMICONSONANTS:			w						j		

VOWELS:

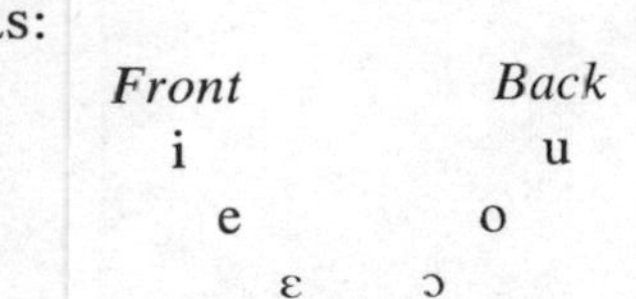

The IPA symbols are aligned vertically according to the place of articulation, and horizontally according to the manner of articulation. The voiceless consonants are at the left, the voiced consonants at the right.

Chart II

COMPARATIVE CHART OF ITALIAN SOUNDS AND THEIR ORDINARY SPELLING

IPA SYMBOLS	ORDINARY SPELLING	EXAMPLES
[ɑ]	a (p. 28)	*a*l*a*
[b]	b (p. 81)	*b*im*b*a
[d]	d (p. 63 and 83)	*d*a*d*o
[dz]	z (p. 92)	*z*elo
[dʒ]	g before *e, i*	*g*ente
	gi before *a, o, u* (p. 93)	*gi*à
[ɛ]	e (p. 19)	*è*
[e]	e (p. 16)	*e*
[f]	f	*f*a
[g]	g before *a, o, u, l, r*	*g*ara
	gh before *e, i* (p. 85 and 93)	la*gh*i
[i]	i (p. 14)	*i*v*i*
[j]	i (p. 102)	p*i*eno
[k]	c before *a, o, u, l, r*	*c*ore
	ch before *e, i* (p. 78 and 93)	*ch*e
[l]	l (p. 55)	a*l*a
[ʎ]	gl before *i*	e*gl*i
	gli before *a, e, o, u* (p. 98)	fi*gli*a
[m]	m	a*m*a
[n]	n (p. 59)	u*n*o
[ɲ]	gn (p. 97)	so*gn*o
[ŋ]	n before *g, k* (p. 62)	a*n*che
[ɔ]	o (p. 26)	n*o*
[o]	o (p. 24)	*o*nta
[p]	p (p. 74)	*p*a*p*a
[ɾ]	r (p. 69)	o*r*o
[r]	r (p. 69)	*r*eo
[s]	s (p. 87)	*s*ei
[ʃ]	sc before *e, i*	*sc*ena
	sci before *a, o, u* (p. 93)	la*sci*a
[t]	t (p. 65 and 76)	*t*e*tt*o
[ts]	z (p. 91)	*z*io
[tʃ]	c before *e, i*	vo*c*e
	ci before *a, o, u* (p. 93)	*ci*an*ci*a
[u]	u (p. 22)	t*u*

Chart II

COMPARATIVE CHART OF ITALIAN SOUNDS AND THEIR ORDINARY SPELLING

IPA SYMBOLS	ORDINARY SPELLING	EXAMPLES
[v]	v	*v*a
[w]	u (p. 103)	*u*omo
[z]	s (p. 89)	*s*mania

Chart III

IPA DIACRITICAL MARKS

['] indicates stress on the following syllable.
[ˌ] indicates secondary stress on the following syllable.
[ː] placed after a vowel indicates that it is long. When two or more vowels share one note in word or phrase, it indicates the vowel which is syllabic and long.
[˘] placed above a vowel indicates that it is very short. When two or more vowels share one note in word or phrase, it indicates the vowel (or vowels) which is nonsyllabic and short.
[ʔ] symbolizes the glottal stop—that is, the glottal attack of a vowel.

Chart IV

IPA SYMBOLS OF ENGLISH SOUNDS

The English vowel sounds are listed in the Introduction.

The following are the English diphthongs and triphthongs mentioned in this book:

IPA SYMBOLS	EXAMPLES
[eɪ̆]	say, eight
[aɪ̆]	high, dry
[oʊ̆]	no, home
[ɑʊ̆]	house, out
[ɪə̆]	dear, cheer
[ɛə̆]	chair, there
[ʊə̆]	poor, tour
[ɔə̆]	or, shore
[aɪ̆ə̆]	fire, lyre
[ɑʊ̆ə̆]	flower, hour

ABBREVIATIONS

adj.	adjective
adv.	adverb
ap.	apocopated, apocopation
f.	feminine
m.	masculine
n.	noun
pl.	plural
poet.	poetic
prep.	preposition
pron.	pronoun
s.	singular
v.	verb

Part I

THE ITALIAN VOWELS

OUTLINE

Italian has five vowel letters—*a, e, i, o* and *u*. These five letters represent seven vowel sounds.

The letter *a* invariably identifies the sound [ɑ] (see Section 3(G)).

The letter *e* may stand either for "close e" [e] or "open e" [ɛ] (see Sections 3(B) and (C)).

With regard to vowel sounds, the letter *i* always symbolizes the sound [i] (see Section 3(A)). Considering the language as a whole, *i* may also stand for the semiconsonant [j] (see Part IV, Section 3). In addition, when following the letters *c, g* or *sc* and preceding *a, o* or *u,* the letter *i* may be silent (see Part III, Section 7).

The letter *o* may identify either "close o" [o] or "open o" [ɔ] (see Sections 3(E) and (F)).

With regard to vowel sounds only, the letter *u* always denotes the sound [u] (see Section 3(D)). Considering the language as a whole, it may also stand for the semiconsonant [w] (see Part IV, Section 4).

1 CHART OF ITALIAN VOWEL SOUNDS

Phoneticians classify vowels according to the position of the tongue.

They organize the seven vowel sounds of the Italian language according to the following chart. (For a comparison with the English chart, see INTRODUCTION, Section 4.)

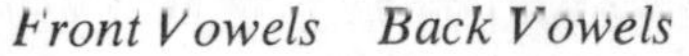

Front Vowels *Back Vowels*

i u

e o

ɛ ɔ

ɑ

Low Vowel

(A) The Three Front Vowels [i] [e] [ɛ]

Front vowels are so called because they require the fronting of the tongue. This means that while the tip of the tongue remains in contact with the lower front teeth, the front of the tongue slides forward and rises toward the hard palate. Accompanying the fronting of the tongue is the spreading of the lips, which is the second characteristic of the front vowels.

A line connecting the [i] with the [ɑ] in the chart would represent the front part of the mouth and tongue. The slanted line indicates that the fronting of the tongue and the spreading of the lips diminish gradually when the vowels are spoken from top to bottom. At the same time, the jaw drops a little with each vowel.

(B) The Three Back Vowels [u] [o] [ɔ]

The back vowels are so called because they require the backing of the tongue. That is, while the tip of the tongue remains in contact with the lower front teeth, the back of the tongue is raised toward the soft palate. Accompanying the backing of the tongue is a marked rounding of the lips, which is the second characteristic of the back vowels.

A line connecting the [u] with the [ɑ] in the chart would represent the back part of the mouth and tongue. Here again the slanting of the line indicates that the backing of the tongue and the rounding of the lips diminish progressively when the vowels are spoken from top to bottom. At the same time the jaw drops a little with each vowel.

(C) The Low Vowel [ɑ]

The low vowel is so called because it is spoken with the tongue in its lowest position. It is neither a front nor a back vowel, since the tongue, neither fronted nor backed, lies flat and relaxed on the floor of the mouth. The lips, neither spread nor rounded, are in a relaxed, neutral position too.

2 CHARACTERISTICS AND GENERAL REMARKS

Before we describe the seven Italian vowel sounds individually, we should discuss some fundamental differences between the English and the Italian vowels.

Italian Vowels Are Always Strong

A main characteristic of English is that the pronunciation of the vowels changes in unstressed syllables and words. English obscures its unstressed vowels; it neutralizes and weakens them.

As an illustration, compare the pronunciation of the letter *a* in *able* (stressed *a*) with the *a* in *syllable* (unstressed *a*); or the *a* in *hard* (stressed *a*) with the *a* in *wizard* (unstressed *a*); or the *o* in *cone* (stressed *o*) with the *o* in *contain* (unstressed *o*).

In each instance, the unstressed vowel is pronounced differently from its corresponding stressed one, and this change in pronunciation is called weakening.

This weakening characteristic of English never occurs in Italian, and it is one of the pitfalls of English-speaking persons singing in Italian.

RULE

Whatever their position in word or phrase, whether stressed or unstressed, alone or combined with one another, Italian vowels maintain their original distinctive acoustic qualities. To an English ear they may sound excessively neat and strong and precise, but that is just how they are supposed to sound.

Italian Monophthongs Prevail Over Diphthongs

Another characteristic of English is its tendency to diphthongize long vowels, particularly long stressed ones. A "diphthong" may be defined as a sequence of two vowel sounds belonging to the same syllable.

Each of the monosyllables *say, I, oil, low, how, dear, air, poor, sour* contains a different diphthong.

The essence of diphthongization lies in starting a vowel with one sound and ending it with another. This is achieved through the shifting of the organs of speech.

Because of the prevalence of diphthongs in English the English-speaking singer tends erroneously to diphthongize the vowels of other languages as well.

Italian is almost at the other extreme of English, since it is characterized by a striking prevalence of "monophthongs."

These are speech sounds which consist of a single vowel sound. For the singer, this predominance of monophthongs is a valuable asset. For a monophthong, unlike a diphthong, is sustained and completed as it was started, without changes and glides of any kind—that is, without interfering movement of the tongue, lips and jaw. All this is of great advantage to the vowel and vocal lines.

Italian, of course, is not completely devoid of diphthongs but compared to English, there are only a few. In addition, Italian diphthongs have the advantage of being spelled phonetically, with two letters representing the two vowel sounds, as in *aura* [ˈɑːŭrɑ] or *feudo* [ˈfɛːŭdɔ]. In other words, in Italian a diphthong is never spelled with a single vowel letter, as in the English words *a, I, no, or*.

Further information concerning Italian diphthongs is contained in Part V. What needs to be stressed here concerning the general characteristics of the Italian vowels is the impressive predominance of its sustained monophthongs and the consequent necessity for a singer to train himself to produce them correctly. Such training will prepare him not only for Italian but also for the many French and German monophthongs. Also it may even help him, in certain instances, to overcome some problems of vocalization.

3 THE SEVEN VOWEL SOUNDS

(A) THE FIRST FRONT VOWEL [i]

DISCUSSION

The Italian first front vowel [i] is identical with the French [i] as in *midi, fini* and with the German [i] as in *Lied, tief*.

It corresponds approximately to the vowel in the English words *see* and *ease*. The difference between the English and the Italian [i] lies in the more pronounced tongue fronting and lip spreading of the Italian vowel.

CLASSIFICATION

The [i] is classified as a "high front vowel," because of the high fronting of the tongue.

SPELLING

The Italian [i] is spelled with the letter *i*.

DIRECTIONS

To say an Italian [i] the jaws should be fairly close to one another but the teeth should not be clenched. The lower jaw should be relaxed and loose.

The lips should be spread, more so than with the English [i], though without tension.

The spreading of the lips should be performed more by the cheek muscles surrounding the lips than by the lips themselves, so that they will be soft and relaxed.

While the tip of the tongue rests in contact with the lower teeth, the tongue is fronted (see Section 1(A)) but more so than with the English [i]. As a result, the sides of the tongue touch the upper front molars and the distance between the fronted tongue and the hard palate is quite small.

REMARK I

The English vowel sound [ɪ] as in *it, him* does not occur in Italian, where each vowel *i* is pronounced [i].

REMARK II

In colloquial English sometimes a diphthong [iə̆] is used in place of a monophthong [i]. This particularly happens when the [i] is final or when it precedes the consonant *l,* as in *sea* or *feel.* The Italian [i] is a monophthong and its timbre—that is, its acoustic quality—will have to be maintained unaltered from beginning to end. This will be achieved if jaw, lips and tongue do not shift their position while the vowel is spoken.

Practicing The First Front Vowel [i]

EXERCISE I

First speak, then sing, long and short [i].

Suggestions And Remarks

For constructive practicing, see INTRODUCTION, Section 6.

a) Sit tall, use a mirror, speak out and listen to yourself.

b) The vowel attack should be clean; that is, the vowel should begin as a neat, definite [i] sound, without the "on-glide" sometimes heard at the beginning of an initial English [i]. A "glide" is an additional transitional sound resulting from speech organs that function too slowly. An on-glide occurs when a vowel is started, while the speech organs are assuming their required position. To avoid an on-glide, they must assume their position before the vowel is started.

c) There is a second requisite for a correct vowel attack; it should not be glottal. The vowel should not start with a little click in the throat, as often heard in colloquial English (see Part VII, Sections 2(B) and (C)). With this in mind, precede the vowel with a very short *h* sound. Even thinking of an *h* without actually saying it will help avoid a glottal attack.

d) Finally, a clean release of the vowel is as important as a clean attack. This means that there should be no "off-glide"—that is, there should be no audible change in the timbre of the vowel at the instant of its release. This will be achieved if the position of the speech organs is maintained for an instant beyond the time of phonation.

EXERCISE II

First speak, then sing, the following syllables, sustaining the vowels. The articulation of the consonants should not interfere with the monophthongal quality of the vowels. In other words, avoid on and off-glides.

[bi], [mi], [di], [ti], [li], [fi], [vi], [ni]
[ib], [im], [id], [it], [il], [if], [iv], [in]

EXERCISE III

First speak, then sing, the following words with a well-supported voice and long monophthongs. An unstressed *i* should not be weakened. It should have the same timbre as the stressed *i*.

ivi ['ivi]	vidi ['vidi]	divini [di'vini]
miti ['miti]	vini ['vini]	dipinti [di'pinti]
liti ['liti]	ridi ['ridi]	Iris ['iɾis]
vivi ['vivi]	pini ['pini]	Mimì [mi'mi]
tipi ['tipi]	finiti [fi'niti]	
fili ['fili]	limiti ['limiti]	

Come back to this word list (and the following ones) for added work as soon as you have studied the Italian consonants.

(B) The Second Front Vowel [e]

DISCUSSION

The Italian second front vowel [e], commonly called "close e," occurs also in French (*été, épée*) and in German (*See, Meer*).

In English a monophthongal [e] may be found only in unstressed syllables, as in the first syllable of *chaotic, vacation*. When stressed, the [e] appears solely as the first vowel of the diphthong [eĭ], as in *rain, veil*.

Since no long stressed monophthong [e] exists in English, it is essential that English-speaking singers acquire this characteristic Italian, French and German sound.

CLASSIFICATION

The [e] is classified as a "half high front vowel," since the tongue is less fronted than when pronouncing the high front vowel [i].

SPELLING

The Italian [e] is spelled with the letter *e*.

DIRECTIONS

To say the sound [e], drop the jaw slightly more than with [i]. Care should be taken that it be loose and relaxed and that the teeth be unclenched.

The lips, only a little less spread than with [i], should be soft and passive, the spreading being performed rather by the surrounding cheek muscles than by the lips themselves.

While the tip of the tongue remains in contact with the lower front teeth, the tongue is fronted, though a little less so than when pronouncing [i]. As a result, the distance between the fronted tongue and the hard palate is increased a little. The sides of the tongue are in contact with the upper front molars.

In proceeding from [i] to [e], the muscular adjustment is complex but minute.

MEANING OF THE TERM "close e"

The term "close e" is justified because this vowel requires a smaller mouth opening than the third front vowel [ɛ], which in contrast is called "open e" (see Section (C)). But the word "close" should not convey any tightness or edge in the vowel sound. To avoid this frequent error, one should relax the jaw and tongue, use a well-supported voice, and think of closing and focussing the vowel high in the resonance chambers.

REMARK

Since the Italian [e] is a monophthong, whether it is long or short, it should be emphasized that it must sound like the simple, undiphthongized sound it is.

Practicing The Second Front Vowel [e]

EXERCISE I

Speak, then sing, long and short [e].

Suggestions And Remarks

a) Sit tall, use a well-supported voice and listen to yourself.

b) The use of the mirror is of particular importance with this sound, since it will be monophthongal only if the jaw, lips and tongue do not shift while the [e] is spoken.

c) For a clean attack without on-glide, the speech organs must be in the required position before the vowel is started.

d) To avoid a glottal attack, precede the vowel with a very short *h* sound.

e) Pay attention to the release of the [e], to avoid the English diphthong [eĭ]. At the instant of its release, the [e] should sound as it did at the moment of its attack. It will, provided you do not shift your speech organs until after the vowel is concluded.

EXERCISE II

Alternate [i] with [e], sustaining the vowels and taking a breath before each one.

EXERCISE III

Speak, then sing, the following syllables, using long vowels and without letting the consonants interfere with the monophthongal quality of the vowel.

[be], [pe], [de], [te], [le], [ne], [fe], [ve],
[eb], [ep], [ed], [et], [el], [en], [ef], [ev].

EXERCISE IV

Speak, then sing, using the same technique:

me ['me]	velo ['velɔ]
sè ['se]	lamento [lɑ'mentɔ]
re ['re]	promessa [prɔ'messɑ]
egli ['eʎi]	casetta [kɑ'zettɑ]
ella ['ellɑ]	vendetta [vɛn'dettɑ]
essi ['essi]	vergine ['verdʒinɛ]
spesso ['spessɔ]	benedetto [bɛnɛ'dettɔ]
pena ['penɑ]	poveretta [pɔvɛ'ɾettɑ]
dentro ['dentrɔ]	carnefice [kɑr'nefitʃɛ]
mentre ['mentrɛ]	Musetta [mu'zettɑ]
trenta ['trentɑ]	Masetto [mɑ'zettɔ]
fresco ['freskɔ]	Violetta [viɔ'lettɑ]
fretta ['frettɑ]	Nannetta [nɑn'nettɑ]
questo ['kwestɔ]	Contessa [kɔn'tessɑ]
tela ['telɑ]	Principessa [printʃi'pessɑ]

EXERCISE V

Practice the following words, reading across from left to right. Differentiate carefully between the first and the second front vowels, since they identify otherwise identical words.

Cina ['tʃinɑ] *China*	cena ['tʃenɑ] *supper*
vile ['vilɛ] *coward*	vele ['velɛ] *sails* (n.)
fitta ['fittɑ] *sharp pain*	fetta ['fettɑ] *slice* (n.)
pinna ['pinnɑ] *fin*	penna ['pennɑ] *pen*
vizzo ['vittsɔ] *withered*	vezzo ['vettsɔ] *habit, charm*
stilla ['stillɑ] *drop* (n.)	stella ['stellɑ] *star* (n.)
vinti ['vinti] *vanquished*	venti ['venti] *twenty*
fritta ['frittɑ] *fried*	fretta ['frettɑ] *hurry* (n.)
pira ['piɾɑ] *pyre*	pera ['peɾɑ] *pear*
affitto [ɑf'fittɔ] *rent* (n.)	affetto [ɑf'fettɔ] *I slice*

Additional Suggestions For Learning The [e] Sound

Because the monophthong [e] is a difficult sound to acquire for most English-speaking persons, the following technique may prove helpful if a singer has difficulty in producing the sound when following normal directions.

1) Say a long [i] following the Directions in Section (A).

2) Say the same sound [i] again, but this time drop your jaw and tongue wide as if yawning. The jaw and tongue must be relaxed, and the tip of the tongue must stay in contact with the lower teeth.

If you succeed in following directions, the vowel resulting from this open mouth position will not sound like a well-enunciated [i], but should instead have the timbre of a monophthongal [e].

In case of difficulty, try to say

1) the English word *bed,* sustaining the vowel;

2) the word *bid,* again sustaining the vowel;

3) a new word, starting with *b* and ending with *d,* but using a vowel in between the vowels of *bed* and *bid.* What you should be saying is a monophthongal [e].

Try the same technique with *let* and *lit, mess* and *miss.*

NOTE

A number of Italian dictionaries and text books use an acute accent over the letter *e* (*é*) to symbolize a "close e."

(C) The Third Front Vowel [ɛ]

DISCUSSION

The Italian third front vowel [ɛ], commonly called "open e," also occurs in English (*pet, said*), in French (*mère, neige*) and in German (*Herz, schnell*).

CLASSIFICATION

The [ɛ] is classified as a "half low front vowel," since the tongue, less fronted, lies lower than when pronouncing the second front vowel [e].

SPELLING

The Italian [ɛ] is spelled with the letter *e.* The sound [e] is also spelled with an *e.* Therefore, in Italian the letter *e* is unphonetic: it corresponds to two sounds, [e] or [ɛ].

DIRECTIONS

To say [ɛ], the jaw is dropped farther than with [e], in a relaxed fashion, and the lips are less spread. While the tip of the tongue remains in contact with the lower teeth, the tongue is fronted, though less so than with [e]. As a consequence, the space between the front of the tongue and the hard palate has increased and the sides of the tongue are not in contact with the upper molars.

REMARK I

If one alternates [e] and [ɛ] in front of a mirror, one will see why the first is called close and the second open. The [ɛ] requires a wider mouth opening than the [e].

REMARK II

In English the vowel [ɛ] occurs either as a short monophthong (*bless, head*) or as the first long vowel of the diphthong [ɛə̆] (*care, there*). This diphthong does not occur in Italian and should not be substituted for the long Italian monophthong [ɛ].

Practicing The Third Front Vowel [ɛ]

EXERCISE I

Speak, then sing, short and long [ɛ].

For a clean release without off-glide, as in the English diphthong [ɛə̆] (as in *chair*), do not move your speech organs for an instant beyond the duration of the vowel.

EXERCISE II

Alternate [e] and [ɛ], using long monophthongs and taking a breath before each one.

EXERCISE III

Practice the progression [i], [e], [ɛ] in the same fashion. In the mirror observe how the jaw drops and the tongue-fronting and lip-spreading diminish as you proceed from the first front vowel to the second and from the second front vowel to the third.

EXERCISE IV

Practice the progression [ɛ], [e], [i] in the same way.

EXERCISE V

Speak, then sing, using long monophthongs:

[lɛ], [nɛ], [bɛ], [pɛ], [dɛ], [tɛ], [vɛ], [sɛ], [zɛ],
[ɛl], [ɛn], [ɛb], [ɛp], [ɛd], [ɛt], [ɛv], [ɛs], [ɛz]

EXERCISE VI

Speak, then sing, sustaining the vowels and giving every [ɛ], stressed or unstressed, its full, unweakened sound:

è ['ɛ]	esse ['ɛssɛ] (letter *s*)	finestra [fi'nɛstrɑ]
tè ['tɛ]	egro ['ɛgrɔ]	ameno [ɑ'mɛnɔ]
deh ['dɛ]	bene ['bɛnɛ]	estasi ['ɛstɑzi]
ero ['ɛɾɔ]	gelo ['dʒɛlɔ]	eterno [ɛ'tɛrnɔ]
eco ['ɛkɔ]	stelo ['stɛlɔ]	estremo [ɛ'strɛmɔ]
erba ['ɛrbɑ]	mesta ['mɛstɑ]	esile ['ɛzilɛ]
estro ['ɛstrɔ]	lieve ['ljɛvɛ]	esule ['ɛzulɛ]
enne ['ɛnnɛ] (letter *n*)	fiero ['fjɛɾɔ]	celeste [tʃɛ'lɛstɛ]
erre ['ɛrrɛ] (letter *r*)	fratello [frɑ'tɛllɔ]	Desdemona [dɛ'zdɛmɔnɑ]
	sorella [sɔ'ɾɛllɑ]	Amneris [ɑm'nɛɾis]
		Amelia [ɑ'mɛljɑ] *

EXERCISE VII

Practice the following words reading across from left to right. Differentiate carefully between the second and the third front vowels, since they identify words that are spelled alike.

esse ['essɛ] *they* (f. pl.)	esse ['ɛssɛ] letter *s*
pesca ['peskɑ] *fishing*	pesca ['pɛskɑ] *peach*
pera ['peɾɑ] *pear*	pera ['pɛɾɑ] *may he perish*
tema ['temɑ] *fear*	tema ['tɛmɑ] *theme*
affetta [ɑf'fettɑ] *he slices*	affetta [ɑf'fɛttɑ] *he affects*

EXERCISE VIII

Reading across from left to right, differentiate with care between the first, second and third front vowels.

vinti ['vinti] *vanquished*	venti ['venti] *twenty*	venti ['vɛnti] *winds*
pira ['piɾɑ] *pyre*	pera ['peɾɑ] *pear*	pera ['pɛɾɑ] *may he perish*
ditte ['dittɛ] *firms*	dette ['dettɛ] *said* (f. pl.)	dette ['dɛttɛ] *he gave*
affitto [ɑf'fittɔ] *rent*	affetto [ɑf'fettɔ] *I slice*	affetto [ɑf'fɛttɔ] *affection*
misto ['mistɔ] *mixture*	mesto ['mestɔ] *I stir*	mesto ['mɛstɔ] *sad*

* See Appendix III.

Additional Suggestions For Learning The [ɛ] Sound

It is not difficult for English-speaking singers to learn how to pronounce the Italian [ɛ], since it is a sound they use in their own language, as in *egg* and *bed*. But sometimes the Italian [ɛ] is spoken and sung too open, more like the English [æ] in *apple,* than the [ɛ] in *debt*. This error often arises with singers who have not yet mastered the "close e" and open it too much. In order to differentiate between [e] and [ɛ], they may overopen the [ɛ] too.

If this is the case, it would be best to practice the "close e" again and improve one's auditory concept of this sound.

NOTE

Some Italian dictionaries and text books use a grave accent above the letter *e* (*è*), to symbolize the "open e."

(D) The First Back Vowel [u]

DISCUSSION

The Italian first back vowel [u] is identical with the German [u] (*du, Blume*).

It is similar to the vowel heard in colloquial English (*do, blue*). The difference between the English and the Italian [u] lies in the more vigorous tongue backing and lip rounding and protruding of the Italian sound.

CLASSIFICATION

The [u] is classified as a "high back vowel" because of the high backing of the tongue.

SPELLING

In Italian, [u] is spelled with the letter *u*.

DIRECTIONS

To say an Italian [u], the jaws should be fairly close to one another, though not clenched. There should be no tightness in the lower jaw.

The lips should protrude, and should be rounded in so small a circle (not a horizontal oval) that the lip corners disappear. The rounding and protruding should be brought about more by the action of the surrounding cheek muscles than by the lips themselves, which should stay soft and relaxed.

The tip of the tongue rests in contact with the lower front teeth, while the back of the tongue is energetically raised toward the soft palate, so that it leaves a narrow space between the two.

MEANING OF THE TERM BACK VOWELS

Since vowel sounds are classified according to the position of the tongue, the term back vowel refers to the tongue position only. It implies that in speaking such a vowel the tongue should be backed. It does not indicate that the vowel should be spoken in the back of the mouth, near the throat.

With all Italian vowels, front, back and low, one should have a sensation of forward resonance—a sensation of resonance "in the mask," as the old Italian maestri used to say. Keeping the tip of the tongue in contact with the lower teeth will help to develop this forward sensation.

REMARK I

The English vowel sound [ʊ], as in *good, look,* does not exist in Italian, where every *u* is pronounced [u].

REMARK II

In conversational English a diphthong [uə̆] is sometimes used in place of a monophthong [u]. This usually happens when the [u] is final, or precedes an *l,* as in *true* or *cool.* Care should be taken that this does not happen in Italian, where every [u] is monophthongal. A monophthong will result if the jaw, lips and tongue do not shift position during the duration of the vowel, or even an instant beyond.

Practicing The First Back Vowel [u]

EXERCISE I

Speak, then sing, long and short [u]. Refer to Section (A), Exercise I.

EXERCISE II

Speak, then sing, using long vowels:

[bu], [mu], [du], [nu], [lu], [ʃu], [ʒu], [vu],
[ub], [um], [ud], [un], [ul], [uʃ], [uʒ], [uv]

The consonants should not interfere with the monophthongal quality of the [u].

EXERCISE III

Speak, then sing, without weakening the unstressed vowels:

tu [ˈtu]	uscio [ˈuʃɔ]	lume [ˈlumɛ]
giù [ˈdʒu]	urlo [ˈurlɔ]	muto [ˈmutɔ]
uno [ˈunɔ]	luna [ˈlunɑ]	cruda [ˈkrudɑ]

frusta ['frustɑ]	unico ['unikɔ]	funebre ['funɛbrɛ]
giuro ['dʒuɾɔ]	ululo ['ululɔ]	furore [fu'ɾoɾɛ]
stupito [stu'pitɔ]	virtù [vir'tu]	Turiddu [tu'ɾiddu]
umile ['umilɛ]	fanciulla [fɑn'tʃullɑ]	Nabucco [nɑ'bukkɔ]
udire [u'diɾɛ]	crudele [kru'dɛlɛ]	Ulrica [ul'rikɑ]

(E) The Second Back Vowel [o]

DISCUSSION

The Italian second back vowel [o], commonly called "close o," also occurs in French (*beau, røse*) and German (*Not, Wohl*).

In English the monophthong [o] occurs in unstressed syllables (*obey, molest*). When stressed, the [o] is found only as the first vowel of the diphthong [oŭ], as in *home, cloak.*

Since no long stressed monophthong [o] exists in English, English-speaking singers should practice this characteristic Italian, French and German sound.

CLASSIFICATION

The [o] is classified as a "half high back vowel," since the tongue is less backed than when pronouncing the high back vowel [u].

SPELLING

The Italian [o] is spelled with the letter *o.*

DIRECTIONS

To say [o], the jaw drops lower than when saying [u], while the lips stay almost as closely rounded and protruded, without tension.

The tip of the tongue rests in contact with the lower teeth; the tongue is backed, though a little less so than with [u]. As a result the space between the back of the tongue and the soft palate has increased.

The muscular adjustments in proceeding from [u] to [o] are minute, except for a marked dropping of the jaw.

REMARK

Since the Italian [o] is a monophthong, whether it is long or short, it should be emphasized that it must sound like the simple, undiphthongized sound it is.

One should avoid the groping movement made by the lips at the end of the English [oŭ] diphthong, for a monophthong will result only if the lips stay in the same position from beginning to end.

PRACTICING THE SECOND BACK VOWEL [o]

EXERCISE I

Speak, then sing, short and long [o].

EXERCISE II

Alternate [u] with [o], sustaining the vowels and taking a breath before each one.

EXERCISE III

Speak, then sing, sustaining the vowels, without letting the consonants interfere with the monophthongal quality of the vowels:

[lo], [mo], [do], [to], [ko], [go], [zo], [so], [fo]
[ol], [om], [od], [ot], [ok], [og], [oz], [os], [of]

EXERCISE IV

Speak, then sing, using the same technique:

onda ['ondɑ]
onta ['ontɑ]
ombra ['ombrɑ]
dono ['donɔ]
dolce ['doltʃɛ]
stolto ['stoltɔ]
molto ['moltɔ]
mondo ['mondɔ]
voce ['votʃɛ]
bocca ['bokkɑ]
conte ['kontɛ]
forse ['forsɛ]
mostro ['mostrɔ]
amore [ɑ'moɾɛ]
dolore [dɔ'loɾɛ]
ardore [ɑr'doɾɛ]
dottore [dɔt'toɾɛ]
canzone [kan'tsonɛ]
superiore [supɛ'ɾjoɾɛ]
Rodolfo [rɔ'dolfɔ]
Gioconda [dʒɔ'kondɑ]
Trovatore [trɔvɑ'toɾɛ]
Borsa ['borsɑ]
Sciarrone [ʃɑr'ronɛ]

EXERCISE V

Practice the following words, reading across from left to right. Carefully differentiate between the first and second back vowels, since they identify otherwise identical words.

uve ['uvɛ] *grapes*	ove ['ovɛ] *where*
unta ['untɑ] *greased* (f.s.)	onta ['ontɑ] *shame* (n.)
urlo ['urlɔ] *scream* (n.)	orlo ['orlɔ] *hem* (n.)
duna ['dunɑ] *dune*	dona ['donɑ] *he gives*
fuga ['fugɑ] *escape* (n.)	foga ['fogɑ] *vehemence*
urna ['urnɑ] *urn*	orna ['ornɑ] *he adorns*

multa ['multɑ] *fine* (n.) molta ['moltɑ] *much* (f. s.)
punte ['puntɛ] *peaks* ponte ['pontɛ] *bridge*
culto ['kultɔ] *cult* colto ['koltɔ] *learned* (adj.)
fusti ['fusti] *stalks* (n.) fosti ['fosti] *you were*

ADDITIONAL SUGGESTIONS FOR LEARNING THE [o] SOUND

Should you find it difficult to learn the monophthongal [o] when following the given directions, try to say:

1) the English word *boot,* prolonging the vowel;

2) then the word *bought,* again prolonging the vowel;

3) finally a new word, starting with *b,* ending with *t,* but using a vowel in between the vowels of *boot* and *bought*. What you should be saying is a monophthongal [o].

Try the same with *fool* and *fall, drew* and *draw*.

NOTE

A number of Italian dictionaries and text books use an acute accent above the letter *o* (*ó*), to symbolize the "close o."

(F) THE THIRD BACK VOWEL [ɔ]

DISCUSSION

The Italian third back vowel [ɔ], commonly called "open o," is identical with the German *o* in *Gott, Wort*.

The difference between Italian and conversational English [ɔ] lies in the certain lax and somewhat spread quality of the latter; whereas the Italian [ɔ] is neat, well placed and spoken with the lips more vertically shaped (see Directions).

CLASSIFICATION

The [ɔ] is known as a "half low back vowel," since the tongue is less backed than when pronouncing the half high back vowel [o].

SPELLING

The Italian [ɔ] is spelled with the letter *o*. The sound [o] is also spelled with an *o*. Therefore, in Italian the letter *o* is unphonetic, pronounced [o] or [ɔ].

DIRECTIONS

To say an Italian [ɔ], the jaw drops much lower than with [o], so as to allow the lips to assume the shape of a distinctly vertical oval. In such an oval, the distance between the upper and lower lip should be much greater than that between the corners of the mouth. The vertical oval will give the [ɔ] its correct sonority.

It will prove helpful to pinch one's cheeks with the thumb and forefinger of one hand near the region of the wisdom teeth. This will cause the jaws to separate and, at the same time, will shape the mouth in the vertical oval position while the lips remain soft and relaxed.

The lips should still protrude a little, though much less than with [u] and [o].

The tip of the tongue stays in contact with the lower front teeth. The tongue is backed, but less so than with the [o], so that the space between the back of the tongue and the soft palate has increased.

In proceeding from [o] to [ɔ], the muscular adjustment of the speech organs is considerable.

REMARK I

If one alternates [o] and [ɔ] in front of a mirror, one will see why the first is called close and the second open. The [ɔ] requires a much wider mouth opening than the [o].

REMARK II

Do not substitute the English diphthong [ɔə̆], sometimes heard colloquially in such words as *law* or *thought* for the Italian monophthong [ɔ]. Keep the jaw, lips and tongue motionless until the vowel is completed, or even an instant beyond, to avert this error.

Practicing The Third Back Vowel [ɔ]

EXERCISE I

Speak, then sing, short and long [ɔ].

EXERCISE II

Alternate [o] and [ɔ], taking a breath before each vowel.

EXERCISE III

Speak, then sing, the progressions [u], [o], [ɔ], and [ɔ], [o], [u] in the same fashion.

EXERCISE IV

Speak, then sing, using prolonged monophthongs:

[lɔ], [nɔ], [ʃɔ], [tʃɔ], [ʒɔ], [dʒɔ], [zɔ], [dzɔ],
[ɔl], [ɔn], [ɔʃ], [ɔtʃ], [ɔʒ], [ɔdʒ], [ɔz], [ɔdz]

EXERCISE V

Speak, then sing, sustaining the vowels and giving every [ɔ], stressed or unstressed, its full unweakened sound:

oh ['ɔ]	morte ['mɔrtɛ]	figliola [fi'ʎɔlɑ]
ho ['ɔ]	gote ['gɔtɛ]	Tonio ['tɔnjɔ]
no ['nɔ]	orrido ['ɔrridɔ]	Antonio [an'tɔnjɔ]
po' ['pɔ]	ristoro [ri'stɔɾɔ]	Lola ['lɔlɑ]
odo ['ɔdɔ]	alloro [ɑl'lɔɾɔ]	Floria ['flɔɾjɑ]
oro ['ɔɾɔ]	tesoro [tɛ'zɔɾɔ]	Flora ['flɔɾɑ]
oste ['ɔstɛ]	solito ['sɔlitɔ]	Goro ['gɔɾɔ]
loco ['lɔkɔ]	morbido ['mɔrbidɔ]	Lindoro [lin'dɔɾɔ]
poco ['pɔkɔ]	povero ['pɔvɛɾɔ]	Leonora [lɛɔ'nɔɾɑ]

EXERCISE VI

Practice the following words, reading across from left to right. Differentiate with care between the second and third back vowels, since they identify words that are spelled alike.

botte ['bottɛ] *barrel*	botte ['bɔttɛ] *blows* (n.)
voto ['votɔ] *vow* (n.)	voto ['vɔtɔ] *empty*
colto ['koltɔ] *learned* (adj.)	colto ['kɔltɔ] *picked*
tosco ['toskɔ] *Tuscan*	tosco ['tɔskɔ] *poison*
torre ['torrɛ] *tower*	torre ['tɔrrɛ] *to take away* (poet.)
torta ['tortɑ] *cake*	torta ['tɔrtɑ] *crooked*
volto ['voltɔ] *face* (n.)	volto ['vɔltɔ] *I turn*
corso ['korsɔ] *course*	corso ['kɔrsɔ] *Corsican*
accorsi [ɑk'korsi] *I ran up*	(mi) accorsi [ɑk'kɔrsi] *I realized*

NOTE

A number of Italian dictionaries and text books use a grave accent above the letter *o* (*ò*), to symbolize the "open o."

(G) The Low Vowel [ɑ]

DISCUSSION

The Italian low vowel [ɑ] is identical with the German low vowel (*Saal, Rast*).

English and American speech uses low vowels which are different from the Italian one.

The Italian low vowel may be described as a natural, relaxed sound, as the vowel most infants use when they babble.

CLASSIFICATION

The Italian [ɑ] is classified as a "low central vowel" since the tongue lies low on the floor of the mouth, without any fronting or backing.

SPELLING

In Italian, [ɑ] is spelled with the letter *a*.

DIRECTIONS

To say [ɑ], the jaw drops comfortably, without effort or tension. The lips, neither spread nor rounded, are at rest and relaxed.

The tongue, also fully relaxed, lies low, limp and flat on the floor of the mouth. As a consequence, it is spread out, so that not only the tip, but the whole anterior part, is in contact with the lower bite.

Practicing The Low Vowel [ɑ]

EXERCISE I

Speak, then sing, long and short [ɑ].

EXERCISE II

Practice the progressions [i], [e], [ɛ], [ɑ] and [ɑ], [ɛ], [e], [i], pausing and taking a breath before each vowel.

EXERCISE III

Do the same with the progressions [u], [o], [ɔ], [ɑ], and [ɑ], [ɔ], [o], [u].

EXERCISE IV

Speak, then sing, with long monophthongs:

[kɑ], [gɑ], [tʃɑ], [dʒɑ], [tsɑ], [dzɑ], [ʃɑ], [zɑ]
[ɑk], [ɑg], [ɑtʃ], [ɑdʒ], [ɑts], [ɑdz], [ɑʃ], [ɑz]

EXERCISE V

Speak, then sing, with long, unweakened vowels:

ala ['ɑlɑ]
ama ['ɑmɑ]
bada ['bɑdɑ]
fata ['fɑtɑ]
cara ['kɑɾɑ]
landa ['lɑndɑ]

madre ['mɑdrɛ]
dama ['dɑmɑ]
basta ['bɑstɑ]
lascia ['lɑʃɑ]
sbaglia ['zbɑʎɑ]
bimba ['bimbɑ]

La Scala = most famous Opera house

amami ['amami]
aita [a'ita]
abito ['abitɔ]
amaro [a'marɔ]
angoscia [aŋ'gɔʃa]
arido ['aridɔ]
fantasma [fan'tazma]
caviglia [ka'viʎa]
candida ['kandida]

Falstaff ['falstaff]
Traviata [travi'ata]
Cavaradossi [kavara'dɔssi]
Attavanti [atta'vanti]
Azucena [adzu'tʃɛna]
Gilda ['dʒilda]
Barnaba ['barnaba]
Aida [a'ida]
Amonasro [amɔ'nazrɔ]

[a]-[ʌ]
don't drop final vowels

Comparative Remarks On [ɔ] And [a]

Some English-speaking singers tend to confuse the third back vowel with the low vowel. They spread the [ɔ] to the point of losing its vertical acoustic identity, while sounding a too dark, or throaty [a]. As a result, the two vowels sometimes sound close to one another, which they should not.

The [ɔ] and [a] are distinct sounds, each with its own characteristics. As a back vowel the [ɔ] requires tongue backing and a pronounced vertical lip oval, whereas the low vowel [a] is produced with a low-lying tongue and the lips in a neutral position.

To give each sound its identifying characteristics, it is helpful, at the beginning, to stress the "vertical oval" lip formation of the [ɔ] and to adopt a smiling, "horizontal oval" lip shape for the [a].

The following practice words contain [ɔ] and [a] sounds. Speak, then sing, differentiating carefully.

caro ['karɔ]
mora ['mɔra]
fola ['fɔla]
foglia ['fɔʎa]
gota ['gɔta]
fato ['fatɔ]
amo ['amɔ]
manto ['mantɔ]
amano ['amanɔ]
tavola ['tavɔla]
compagna [kɔm'paɲa]
camino [ka'minɔ]

madonna [ma'dɔnna]
ancora ['aŋkɔra]
soave [sɔ'avɛ]
somaro [sɔ'marɔ]
corallo [kɔ'rallɔ]
sgorgava [zgɔr'gava]
Lola ['lɔla]
Alvaro [al'varɔ]
Bartolo ['bartɔlɔ]
Amonasro [amɔ'nazrɔ]
Giovanna [dʒɔ'vanna]
Fontana [fɔn'tana]

all final o are open [ɔ]

Part II

THE ITALIAN VOWELS IN LYRIC DICTION

INTRODUCTION

Having discussed the seven vowel sounds, we will now provide the rules for the use of each sound in lyric diction.

The rules applying to lyric diction do not necessarily apply to conversation. There are phonetic differences between the way in which a language is spoken colloquially and the manner in which it should be sung. The increased voice range, the intensified tone power and resonance, and the unnatural duration of the vowels, characteristic of singing, present the singer with special problems.

Italian lyric diction for the most part corresponds to colloquial speech. Sometimes, however, it varies to fulfill the requirements of singing.

In this book, any divergence from colloquial Italian will be pointed out. Unless otherwise stated, lyric diction will correspond to conversational usage.

1 THE THREE PHONETIC VOWELS *a, i, u*

With regard to vowel sounds, the letters *a, i* and *u* are phonetic, for each corresponds to one and the same sound, [ɑ], [i] and [u], respectively. This, however, refers to vowel sounds only. For other possibilities in the pronunciation of *i* and *u* see Part I, Outline.

2 THE TWO UNPHONETIC VOWELS *e* AND *o*

The letters *e* and *o* are unphonetic since each may be either close or open, and consequently identifies two vowel sounds, [e], [ɛ] and [o], [ɔ], respectively.

3 THE CLOSING AND OPENING OF *e* AND *o*, ITS SIGNIFICANCE AND IMPORTANCE

Italian spelling does not indicate the closing or opening of the letters *e* and *o*. Yet it is essential that these vowels be pronounced correctly for esthetic as well as practical reasons.

There are only seven Italian vowel sounds as compared to the fourteen German, fifteen English and sixteen French ones. When foreigners, or natives speaking with regional accents, fail to differentiate between the close and open *e* and *o,* they are using five vowel sounds instead of seven. Thus they distort the sound pattern of the language, by depriving it of its characteristic sonority.

From a practical standpoint, one who does not differentiate between close and open *e* and *o* will find it difficult to make himself understood, since many Italian words with identical spelling have different meanings, depending solely on the closing or opening of the stressed *e* or *o.*

Practice speaking and singing, reading across the page from left to right:

affetto [ɑf'fettɔ] *I slice*	affetto [ɑf'fɛttɔ] *affection*
esca ['eskɑ] *bait* (n.)	esca ['ɛskɑ] *may he go out*
mesto ['mestɔ] *I mix*	mesto ['mɛstɔ] *sad*
venti ['venti] *twenty*	venti ['vɛnti] *winds*
fosse ['fossɛ] *if he were*	fosse ['fɔssɛ] *ditches*
porsi ['porsi] *to put oneself*	porsi ['pɔrsi] *I offered*
sorta ['sortɑ] *arisen* (f. s.)	sorta ['sɔrtɑ] *kind* (n.)
corre ['korrɛ] *he runs*	corre ['kɔrrɛ] *to pick* (poet.)

Since the spelling does not indicate the pronunciation of *e* or *o,* it is the context which will suggest the correct choice of sounds, just as with the English *read* (present) and *read* (past) or *wind* (noun) and *wind* (verb).

4 THREE BASIC RULES FOR THE PRONUNCIATION OF *e* AND *o* IN LYRIC DICTION

According to its position within a word, a sound may be termed initial, medial or final. In the word *amore,* for instance, the *a* is initial, the *e* is final and the *m, o, r* are medial.

RULE I

In lyric diction, final *e* or *o* is open, although this is not true of conversational Italian (see Appendix 1).

padre ['pɑdrɛ]	caro ['kɑɾɔ]
forte ['fɔrtɛ]	bambino [bɑm'binɔ]
lagrime ['lɑgrimɛ]	splendido ['splɛndidɔ]
amore [ɑ'moɾɛ]	adorerò [ɑdɔɾɛ'ɾɔ]

RULE II

In lyric diction, the unstressed *e*'s and *o*'s in a polysyllable (a word of more than one syllable) are also open. This again is not true of colloquial Italian (see Appendix I).

respiro [rɛ'spirɔ]
verace [vɛ'ratʃɛ]
benedetto [bɛnɛ'dettɔ]
estremo [ɛ'strɛmɔ]

fortuna [fɔr'tuna]
condannato [kɔndan'natɔ]
incoronare [iŋkɔrɔ'narɛ]
sfolgorante [sfɔlgɔ'rantɛ]

RULE III

In lyric diction, as in conversation, the remaining *e*'s and *o*'s, which comprise all those neither final nor unstressed in a polysyllable, may be either close or open.

DISCUSSION

There are no rules to indicate how the above *e*'s and *o*'s should be pronounced. Essentially the *e*'s and *o*'s of Rule III are pronounced according to established usage which has resulted from the manner in which the Italian language evolved from Latin.

In the following examples, either identically or similarly spelled Italian words have been put side by side to show that there is no norm for the closing or opening of the *e*'s and *o*'s of Rule III. To be certain that the right word and its correct pronunciation are used, one should consult a reputable dictionary (see Appendix IV).

Practice speaking and singing reading across from left to right:

legge ['leddʒɛ] *law*	legge ['lɛddʒɛ] *he reads,* etc.
accetta [at'tʃetta] *axe*	accetta [at'tʃɛtta] *he accepts,* etc.
caminetto [kami'nettɔ] *fireplace*	dispetto [di'spɛttɔ] *spite*
velo ['velɔ] *veil*	gelo ['dʒɛlɔ] *frost*
volgo ['volgɔ] *common people*	volgo ['vɔlgɔ] *I turn*
scopo ['skopɔ] *I sweep*	scopo ['skɔpɔ] *purpose*
amore [a'morɛ] *love* (n.)	core ['kɔrɛ] *heart*
sonno ['sonnɔ] *sleep* (n.)	nonno ['nɔnnɔ] *grandfather*

REMARKS

Since in Italian there is only one stressed syllable and vowel to a word, in lyric diction words will have one close vowel or none at all. As a consequence, open *e*'s and *o*'s greatly outnumber the close ones.

Because the operatic vocabulary is fairly limited, it should be possible, with some diligence and practice, to acquire a useful knowledge of the way in which most of its words are pronounced.

5 THE STRESS OF WORDS AND THE ACCENTS

The Stress Of Words And The Grave Accent

As long as the closing or opening of the *e*'s and *o*'s of Rules II and III depends on the stress of the word, it is essential for correct pronunciation that a singer be able to identify promptly the stressed syllable of a polysyllable.

In Italian the stress of words may fall:

a) on the final vowel, as in *carità* [kɑɾi'tɑ],
b) on the vowel before last, as in *canzone* [kɑn'tsonɛ],
c) on the third vowel from the last, as in *gelida* ['dʒɛlidɑ],
d) on the fourth from the last, as in *strepitano* ['strɛpitɑnɔ].

Other instances are infrequent, and may be ignored for all practical purposes.

Italian spelling indicates stress in only one of the four instances listed above; when the stress falls on the final vowel of a polysyllable. The stress is then indicated by a grave accent (`) over the final vowel.

pietà [pjɛ'tɑ]	fallì [fɑl'li]
virtù [vir'tu]	chiuderò [kjudɛ'ɾɔ]
perchè [pɛr'ke]	rifiorirà [rifjɔɾi'ɾɑ]
caffè [kɑf'fɛ]	manderò [mɑndɛ'ɾɔ]

When a polysyllable has no grave accent on the final vowel, one knows only that the stress does not fall on that vowel. In a word of two syllables ending with a vowel, the stress is obvious. In the word *amò* [ɑ'mɔ] (*he loved*), for instance, the stress falls on the final vowel, whereas in the word *amo* ['ɑmɔ] (*I love*), the stress falls on the first syllable.

But what about words of three or more syllables with no stress-identifying accent on the final vowel? Is there any way of recognizing their stress? Here are three four-syllable words:

mormorano	*they murmur*
amavano	*they used to love*
dolcemente	*sweetly*

The first is stressed on the first syllable, the second on the second syllable, the third on the third syllable. If one is reading an Italian book, one would have to consult a dictionary in order to determine the stress of these words. This is not the case, however, with a text set to music. For, in a text set to music, the well-trained singer will soon discover that in most of the traditional styles the beat of the music corresponds to the stress of the words. As a result, the stress of a polysyllable will be indicated by the beat of the music.

This is not a sacred law, particularly in our own time when composers are discovering new means of expression. However, in most traditional music the stressed syllable of an important word is on a down beat, or a strong beat.

Accordingly, a vocalist whose knowledge of spoken Italian is weak can usually be guided in word stress by rhythmically speaking the text in time with the beat of the music.

To exemplify how the stress of words may be detected through the rhythm of the music, the beginning of the Alessandro Scarlatti aria "Le violette" will be used. The text starts with the following four four-syllable words: "Rugiadose, odorose, violette graziose, . . ." The aria is in 4/4 time, with the main stresses on the first and third beats. This will indicate that the syllable *do,* which falls on the third beat must be, and is, the stressed syllable of the word *rugiadose* [rudʒɑ'dozɛ]; that the syllable *ro* falling on the first beat should be, and is, the stressed syllable of *odorose* [ɔdɔ'ɾozɛ]; that the syllable *let* found on the first beat carries the stress of the word *violette* [viɔ'lettɛ]; and finally that the syllable *o* which is found on the first beat is, as it should be, the stressed syllable of *graziose* [grɑtsi'ozɛ].

Since each of the stressed syllables contains an unphonetic vowel which is neither final (Rule I) nor unstressed (Rule II), we must conclude that, as with all the *e*'s and *o*'s of Rule III, their pronunciation will have to be determined with the help of a dictionary. According to the dictionary all four of these stressed vowels happen to be close. According to Rules I and II all the other *e*'s and *o*'s are open, either because final, or because they are unstressed in a polysyllable. This, then, is the way this phrase should sound:

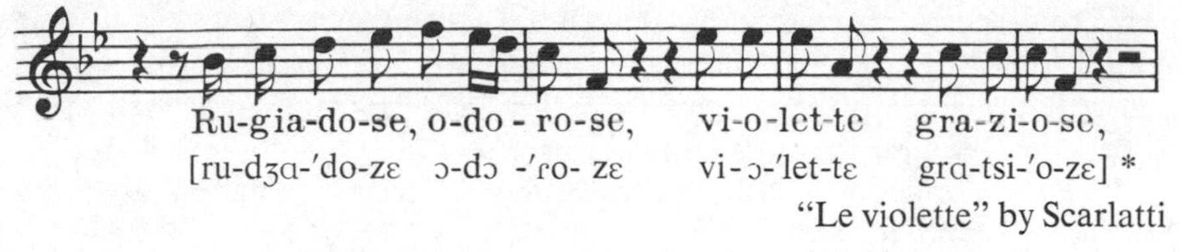

"Le violette" by Scarlatti

More On The Grave Accent

As stated, a grave accent on the final vowel of a polysyllable indicates stress.

There is another instance in which the grave accent is used in Italian; as an identification mark on monosyllables, for it may identify a monosyllable stressed in the phrase from an identically spelled unstressed one.

If, for instance, one comes across the word *sì* ['si] (*yes*), spelled with a grave accent, one should conclude that there must be another monosyllable, also spelled *si* ['si] (*himself*), but without an accent and with a different meaning.

Here is a list of the more frequent, identically spelled, monosyllables: the stressed ones, with a grave accent, are at the left, the unstressed without accent, are at the right.

è ['ɛ] *he is,* etc.	e ['e] *and*
sì ['si] *yes*	si ['si] *himself*
là ['lɑ] *there*	la ['lɑ] *the, her, it*
lì ['li] *there*	li ['li] *them*
tè ['tɛ] *tea*	te ['tɛ] *you* (conjunctive pron.)
dì ['di] *day,* or *say!*	di ['di] *of*

* See Appendix II.

dà ['dɑ] *he gives,* etc. or *give!*	da ['dɑ] *from*
chè ['ke] *for, because*	che ['kɛ] *who, whom, that, which* (relative pron.)
nè ['ne] *neither, nor*	ne ['nɛ] *of it, of them,* etc.
sè ['se] *himself, herself,* etc.	se ['sɛ] *if*

The fact that *è* and *tè* have an open vowel, whereas *chè, nè, sè* have a close one, indicates that there are exceptions to Rule I (final *e* or *o* is open), and that unlike French a grave accent in Italian is not normally indicative of the sound character of the vowel. In the following section some infrequent instances will be discussed where it actually is.

THE ACUTE AND CIRCUMFLEX ACCENTS

Although the grave accent (`) is traditionally the only accent used in Italian, one occasionally finds an acute accent (′), and even a circumflex accent (ˆ).

The reason is that there have been isolated authors who have used an acute accent on close stressed final *e* (exceptions to Rule I). This is not a generally accepted rule; nevertheless one may come across *perché* as well as *perchè* [pɛr'ke], *temé* as well as *temè* [tɛ'me], *sé* as well as *sè* ['se], etc., because the stressed final *e* is close.

No acute accent will be found on final *o,* because final *o*'s are open without exception.

There is another instance where either a grave or an acute accent may be found. This is when there is the need for quickly identifying the stress of a word whose meaning changes with the change of stress. *Àncora* ['ɑŋkɔrɑ], for example, means *anchor,* whereas *ancóra* [ɑŋ'korɑ], means *again.* Since this last *o* is close, a writer wishing to use an accent to convey stress would choose the acute accent in order to indicate at the same time that this stressed *o* is close. The acute or grave accent would then actually denote the pronunciation of the vowel, in addition to indicating the stress of the word. But this rarely happens.

Following are some words whose meanings change with the change of stress. For this special reason they may be written with a grave or acute accent, depending on the pronunciation of the stressed vowel:

pèrdono ['pɛrdɔnɔ] *they lose*	perdóno [pɛr'donɔ] *pardon* (n.)
mèta ['mɛtɑ] *goal*	metà [mɛ'tɑ] *half*
bàlia ['bɑljɑ] *nurse* (n.)	balìa [bɑ'liːɑ] *power*
giòia ['dʒɔjɑ] *joy*	gioìa [dʒɔ'iːɑ] *I used to rejoice, etc.* (poet.)
cólpi ['kolpi] *blows* (n.)	colpì [kɔl'pi] *he hit,* etc.
ìntimo ['intimɔ] *intimate* (adj.)	intìmo [in'timɔ] *I command*
mèrce ['mɛrtʃɛ] *merchandise*	mercé [mɛr'tʃe] *reward, thanks* (ap.)

màrtiri ['mɑrtiɾi] *martyrs* martìri [mɑr'tiɾi] *torments* (n.)
cómpito ['kompitɔ] *assignment* compìto [kɔm'pitɔ] *accomplished* (adj.)

The circumflex accent, however, denotes neither pronunciation nor stress. It may be found occasionally on an unstressed final *i* to signify that the *i* is actually the contraction of two final unstressed *i*'s.

Thus, one may come across the spelling *rimedî* as well as *rimedii* or *rimedi* [ri'mɛdi], or *odî* as well as *odii* or *odi* ['ɔdi]. The pronunciation, however, never varies.

6 ADDITIONAL RULES FOR THE PRONUNCIATION OF *e* AND *o*

(A) THE MONOSYLLABLES *e, ed, è, eh, o, oh, ho,* AND THE LETTERS OF THE ALPHABET *e* AND *o*

The monosyllable *e,* frequently changed to *ed* when preceding a vowel, means *and,* and is close [e], [ed].

The word *è,* spelled with a grave accent, means *is* and is open [ɛ].

The interjection *eh,* equivalent to the English *ah* and expressing various emotions, is open [ɛ].

The fifth letter of the alphabet, *e,* is called by its close sound [e].

The monosyllable *o* has three different meanings. When it corresponds to the English conjunctions *either* and *or,* it may change to *od* in front of a vowel. In addition, the word *o* may be an interjection used in directly addressing the deity, a person or a place, as in *O Lord!* No matter which of these three meanings the Italian *o* has, it should always sound close [o].

The interjection *oh,* which is an exclamation expressing emotions, such as joy, surprise, grief or fear, corresponds to the English *oh* in phrases such as *Oh, how beautiful!* In Italian, *oh* is open [ɔ].

The word *ho,* which means *I have,* is also open [ɔ] (the *h* is silent).

The thirteenth letter of the Italian alphabet, *o,* is called by its open sound [ɔ].

EXAMPLES

. . . e qui la lu-na . . .
[e kwi lɑ 'lu-nɑ]

La Bohème, Act I [1]

[1] In Part VII, Section 3(D) we will see that a word in this and in some of the following examples calls for a phrasal doubling. Until this doubling is explained in Part VII it has been purposely ignored so as to concentrate on the problems at hand.

Ed è bel-la la spo-sa?
[e - dɛ ˈbɛl-lɑ lɑ ˈspɔ-zɑ]

Madama Butterfly, Act I

For-tu-na? eh la fa-rà.
[fɔr-ˈtu-nɑ ɛ lɑ fɑ-ˈɾɑ]

Il barbiere di Siviglia, Act I

O cie-li az-zur-ri . . .
[o tʃɛ-ʎʎjɑd-ˈdzur-ri]

Aida, Act III

Son Tosca! . . . o Scar-pia!!
[son ˈtɔ-skɑ o ˈskɑr-pjɑ]

Tosca, Act II

Que-sta o quel-la . . .
[kwe-stɑ̆oː ˈkwel-lɑ]

Rigoletto, Act I [2]

Oh! sven-ta-ta, sven-ta-ta!
[ˈɔ zvɛn-ˈtɑ-tɑ zvɛn-ˈtɑ-tɑ]

La Bohème, Act I

Oh, co-me è bel-lo . . .
[ˈɔ ko - mɛ ˈbɛl-lɔ]

La Bohème, Act III

[2] For the meaning of [ː] and [˘] see Chart III.

Ho tan-te co-se . . .
[ɔ 'tɑn-tɛ 'kɔ-zɛ]

La Bohème, Act III

(B) The Contractions *del, della,* etc.

When one of the prepositions *di* ['di], *in* ['in], *per* ['pɛr], *con* ['kɔn] is followed by a definite article the two usually contract into a single word. Thus *di* and *il* contract into *del.*

When one of these contractions has a Rule III *e* or *o,* in lyric diction this *e* or *o* is open.

EXAMPLES

del ['dɛl], nell' ['nɛl], pello ['pɛllɔ], colla ['kɔllɑ], etc.

Bel-la fi-glia del-l'a-mo-re, . . .
[bɛl-lɑ 'fi-ʎɑ dɛl-lɑ-'mo-ɾɛ]

Rigoletto, Act III

Nel poz-zo . . . nel giar-di-no . . .
[nɛl 'pot-tsɔ nɛl dʒɑr-'di-nɔ]

Tosca, Act II

. . . via pei li-di, via pel ma-re . . .
['vi:ɑ̆ pɛ:ĭ li-di vi:ɑ̆ pɛl 'mɑ-ɾɛ]

Madama Butterfly, Act I

(C) Apocopated Words With Stressed *e* Or *o*

"Apocopation" is the omission of the unstressed final vowel of a polysyllable, as in *cor* ['kɔr] for *core* ['kɔɾɛ].

Sometimes, though less frequently, the unstressed final syllable is omitted, as with *fra* ['frɑ] for *frate* ['frɑtɛ], *po'* ['pɔ] for *poco* ['pɔkɔ], *vo'* ['vɔ] for *voglio* ['vɔʎɔ].

Poetry and song make more frequent use of apocopation than conversational Italian.

RULE

When an apocopated word has a stressed *e* or *o,* the *e* or *o* maintains the original pronunciation of the unapocopated word. Consequently, the *o* in *amor* [ɑ'mor] is as close as the *o* in *amore* [ɑ'moɾɛ], and the stressed *e* in *velen* [vɛ'len] is as close as the one in *veleno* [vɛ'lenɔ].

EXAMPLES

Dor-mi a-mor(e) mi-o, dor-mi sul mio cor(e).
['dɔr-mjɑ-mor 'mi-ɔ 'dɔr-mi sul mi:ɔ̆ 'kɔr]

Madama Butterfly, Act III

. . . il mio si-gnor(e) con-so-le, . . .
[il mi:ɔ̆ si-ɲor 'kon-sɔ-lɛ]

Madama Butterfly, Act II

Vo'(glio) che mi ve-da in-dos-so il vel(o) . . .
['vɔ kɛ mi 've-dɑ:ĭn-'dɔs-sɔ il 'vel]

Madama Butterfly, Act II

Non è ver(o), . . .
[nɔ - nɛ 'ver]

Tosca, Act II

(D) More On Final *e* And *o*

According to Rule I, final *o* is open, whether accented or unaccented. There are no exceptions.

moro ['mɔɾɔ]	morrò [mɔr'rɔ]
amo ['ɑmɔ]	amò [ɑ'mɔ]
Antonio [ɑn'tɔnjɔ]	no ['nɔ]

Final *e,* accented or unaccented, is also open, but with the following exceptions:

List Of Words With Final Close *e*

(a) *chè* ['ke], sometimes spelled *ché,* a conjunction meaning *for, since,* and its many compounds, all conjunctions, such as:

perchè, sometimes spelled perché [pɛr'ke]
poichè, or poiché [pɔːĭ'ke]
giacchè, or giacché [dʒɑk'ke]
finchè, or finché [fiŋ'ke]
dacchè, or dacché [dɑk'ke]
sicchè, or sicché [sik'ke]

(b) *tre* ['tre], meaning *three,* and its compounds, including:

ventitrè, sometimes spelled ventitré [ˌventi'tre] *
trentatrè, or trentatré [ˌtrentɑ'tre]
quarantatrè, or quarantatré [kwɑˌɾɑntɑ'tre]

(c) All third person singular forms of the past absolute of the regular verbs of the second conjugation, such as:

temè, sometimes spelled temé [tɛ'me]
godè, or godé [gɔ'de]
ripetè, or ripeté [ripɛ'te]

Note, however, that *diè* ['djɛ] (poet. ap. of *diede* ['djɛdɛ], past absolute of *dare*) belongs to the first conjugation and has an open final [ɛ]. It is invariably spelled with a grave accent.

(d) The three stressed disjunctive personal pronouns:

me ['me] *me*
te ['te] *you*
sè, sometimes also spelled sé ['se] *him, himself,* etc.

(e) The following words:

re ['re] *king*
fè, fé ['fe] (ap. of *fede* ['fedɛ]) *faith*

* See Chart III for secondary stress.

affè, affé [ɑf'fe] *upon my faith!*
fé, fe' ['fe] (ap. of *fece* ['fetʃɛ] *he made,* etc.
e' ['e] (ap. of *egli* ['eʎi], *ei* ['e:ĭ]) *he*
mercè, or mercé [mɛr'tʃe] (ap. of *mercede* [mɛr'tʃedɛ]) *reward, thanks*
nè, né ['ne] *neither, nor*

(E) Suffixes And Verb Endings With Stressed *e* Or *o*

To memorize the individual pronunciation of every word with a stressed *e* or *o* would be quite a task. It is easier and more constructive to study the pronunciation of words grouped according to their suffixes.

For example, in English the regular adverbial ending is *-ly,* as in *kindly, promptly.* The corresponding regular adverbial ending in Italian is *-mente,* with a stressed "close e." It is helpful to know that if the stressed *e* in *lentamente* [lɛntɑ'mentɛ], *finalmente* [finɑl'mentɛ] is close it will have to be close in all other adverbs ending in *-mente.*

To facilitate the work of the singer, the more frequently recurring suffixes with a stressed *e* or *o* have been listed below grouped according to the pronunciation of the stressed *e* or *o.*

Suffixes With Stressed Close *e*

-ese ['ezɛ] * (n. or adj.)	inglese [iŋ'glezɛ], francese [frɑn'tʃezɛ]
-essa ['essɑ] (n.)	contessa [kɔn'tessɑ], principessa [printʃi'pessɑ]
-etto ['ettɔ] (n. or adj.)	caminetto [kami'nettɔ], Masetto [mɑ'zettɔ] (diminutives)
-etta ['ettɑ] (n. or adj.)	Violetta [viɔ'lettɑ], Musetta [mu'zettɑ] (diminutives)
-evole ['evɔlɛ] (adj.)	lodevole [lɔ'devɔlɛ], svenevole [zvɛ'nevɔlɛ]
-ezza ['ettsɑ] (n.)	bellezza [bɛl'lettsɑ], fierezza [fjɛ'rettsɑ]
-mente ['mentɛ] (adv.)	gentilmente [dʒɛntil'mentɛ], lentamente [lɛntɑ'mentɛ]
-mento ['mentɔ] (n.)	tormento [tɔr'mentɔ], sentimento [sɛnti'mentɔ]

Verb Endings With Stressed Close *e*

-ere ['erɛ]	Infinitive (2nd Conjugation): *temere* [tɛ'merɛ]
-ete ['etɛ]	Present Indicative and Imperative, 2nd Person Pl. (2nd Conjugation): *temete* [tɛ'metɛ], *temete!* [tɛ'metɛ]
-evo ['evɔ], -evi ['evi], -eva ['evɑ], -evano ['evɑnɔ]	Imperfect Indicative, 1st, 2nd, 3rd Person S. and 3rd Person Pl. (2nd Conjugation): *temevo* [tɛ'mevɔ], *temevi* [tɛ'mevi], *temeva* [tɛ'mevɑ], *temevano* [tɛ'mevɑnɔ]

* See Appendix II.

-ei ['ei], -esti ['esti], -è ['e], -emmo ['emmɔ], -este ['estɛ], -erono ['erɔnɔ]	Past Absolute Indicative, All Persons and Numbers (2nd Conjugation): *temei* [tɛ'mei], *temesti* [tɛ'mesti], *temè* [tɛ'me], *tememmo* [tɛ'memmɔ], *temeste* [tɛ'mestɛ], *temerono* [tɛ'merɔnɔ]
-eremo [ɛ'remɔ] or -iremo [i'remɔ], -erete [ɛ'retɛ], etc.	Future Indicative, 1st and 2nd Person Pl. (All Conjugations): *parleremo* [parlɛ'remɔ], *parlerete* [parlɛ'retɛ]
-eresti [ɛ'resti] or -iresti [i'resti], -eremmo [ɛ'remmɔ], etc. -ereste [ɛ'restɛ], etc.	Present Conditional, 2nd S., and 1st and 2nd Pl. (All Conjugations): *dormiresti* [dɔrmi'resti], *dormiremmo* [dɔrmi'remmɔ], *dormireste* [dɔrmi'restɛ]
-essi ['essi], -essi ['essi], -esse ['essɛ], -essimo ['essimɔ], -este ['estɛ], -essero ['essɛrɔ]	Imperfect Subjunctive, All Persons and Numbers (2nd Conjugation): *temessi* [tɛ'messi], *temessi* [tɛ'messi], *temesse* [tɛ'messɛ], *temessimo* [tɛ'messimɔ], *temeste* [tɛ'mestɛ], *temessero* [tɛ'messɛrɔ]

SUFFIXES WITH STRESSED OPEN *e*

-ello ['ɛllɔ] (n.)	gioiello [dʒɔ'jɛllɔ], campanello [kampa'nɛllɔ]
-ella ['ɛlla] (n.)	damigella [dami'dʒɛlla], facella [fa'tʃɛlla]
-ente ['ɛntɛ] (adj.)	dolente [dɔ'lɛntɛ], languente [laŋ'gwɛntɛ]
-esimo ['ɛzimɔ] (adj.)	centesimo [tʃɛn'tɛzimɔ], millesimo [mil'lɛzimɔ]
-estre ['ɛstrɛ] (adj.)	campestre [kam'pɛstrɛ], silvestre [sil'vɛstrɛ]

VERB ENDINGS WITH STRESSED OPEN *e*

-erei [ɛ'rɛi] or -irei [i'rɛi], -erebbe [ɛ'rɛbbɛ], etc., -erebbero [ɛ'rɛbbɛrɔ], etc.	Present Conditional, 1st and 3rd Person S., and 3rd Person Pl. (All Conjugations): *dormirei* [dɔrmi'rɛːi], *dormirebbe* [dɔrmi'rɛbbɛ], *dormirebbero* [dɔrmi'rɛbbɛrɔ]
-endo ['ɛndɔ]	Present Gerund (2nd and 3rd Conjugation): *temendo* [tɛ'mɛndɔ], *dormendo* [dɔr'mɛndɔ]

SUFFIXES WITH STRESSED CLOSE *o*

-one ['onɛ] (n.)	farfallone [farfal'lonɛ], vallone [val'lonɛ]
-ore ['orɛ] (n. or adj.)	amore [a'morɛ] dolore [dɔ'lorɛ], inferiore [infɛ'rjorɛ]
-oso ['ozɔ] (adj.)	pietoso [pjɛ'tozɔ], glorioso [glɔri'ozɔ]
-zione ['tsjonɛ] (n.)	benedizione [bɛnɛdi'tsjonɛ], maledizione [malɛdi'tsjonɛ]

Suffixes With Stressed Open *o*

-olo ['ɔlɔ] (n.) giaggiolo [dʒɑd'dʒɔlɔ], figliolo [fi'ʎɔlɔ]
-ola ['ɔlɑ] (n.) famigliola [fɑmi'ʎɔlɑ], figliola [fi'ʎɔlɑ]
-otto ['ɔttɔ] (n.) vecchiotto [vɛk'kjɔttɔ], giovinotto [dʒɔvi'nɔttɔ]

(F) Stressed *e* And *o* In Compound Words And In Adverbs Ending In *-mente*

In compound words, the original stress of the first component becomes a secondary stress. Thus, the compound word *sottosopra* [ˌsottɔ'soprɑ] (*topsy-turvy*) has the main stress on the last *o* and, in addition, a secondary stress on the first *o*.

Because of this secondary stress, the original close pronunciation of the first *o* has to be maintained. Thus, this is a rare instance of a word with two stresses and two close vowels.

Secondary stresses on close *e* or *o* occur in other compound words, such as *sottomettere* [ˌsottɔ'mettɛrɛ] (*to subdue*), *dopodomani* [ˌdopɔdɔ'mɑni] (*the day after tomorrow*), *Boccanegra* [ˌbokkɑ'negrɑ] (family name deriving from *bocca* and *negra*).

Similarly, in an adverb ending in *-mente* ['mentɛ], the original stress of the adjective from which the adverb derives becomes a secondary stress. Thus, *dolcemente* [ˌdoltʃɛ'mentɛ], which derives from the adjective *dolce,* has the main stress on the vowel before last and, in addition, a secondary stress on the originally stressed close *o,* which has to maintain its close pronunciation.

A few adverbs thus have two close vowels, including *veramente* [ˌverɑ'mentɛ], *velocemente* [vɛˌlotʃɛ'mentɛ], *atrocemente* [ɑˌtrotʃɛ'mentɛ].

Part III

THE CONSONANTS

INTRODUCTION AND OUTLINE

Consonants are speech sounds characterized by a constriction or stoppage of the flow of breath by some of the articulatory organs, such as the lips, tongue (tip, front or back), teeth, upper gums, hard and soft palate, jaw and vocal cords.

The nature of a consonant is determined by the speech organs involved, by the manner in which the speech organs function and by the activity or inactivity of the vocal cords. Consonants are classified according to these three factors.

Chart I indicates that, according to the organs of speech involved, Italian consonants, as used in singing, may be "bilabial," "labiodental," "dental," "prepalatal" or "mediopalatal." These, and the following terms, will be explained when the consonants to which they apply are discussed.

The same chart indicates that these consonants may be "plosive," "nasal," "lateral," "vibrant," "fricative" or "affricate," according to the manner of articulation.

Finally, we distinguish "voiced" consonants, articulated with accompanying vibrations of the vocal cords, from "unvoiced" ones (also called "voiceless") spoken without vibrations of the vocal cords.

For some fundamental characteristics of Italian consonants, see Sections 1 and 2.

The differences in articulation between certain Italian consonants and their English counterparts are pointed out in Sections 3, 4 and 5, in which the Dentals, the Voiceless Plosives and the Voiced Plosives are discussed respectively.

For the pronunciation of the unphonetic consonants *s* and *z*, see Section 6, and for the pronunciation of *c, g* and *sc,* see Section 7.

Section 8 deals with the Prepalatal Consonants [ɲ] and [ʎ], which do not occur in English, and Section 9 discusses the pronunciation of the letters, *h, j, k, q, w, x* and *y.*

The phonetic consonants *m, f* and *v,* which are pronounced as in English, are listed in Charts I and II but not further discussed.

1 FUNDAMENTAL CHARACTERISTICS OF ITALIAN CONSONANTS

The Basic Tongue Position

If one listens attentively to good Italian speech, one will notice that Italian consonants sound neater, sharper and more precise than their English counterparts. This marked crispness is due to the fact that in Italian the adjusting movements of the speech organs are quicker and more energetic than in English. In addition, they take place farther forward in the mouth.

What is the cause of this heightened articulatory alertness?

If one observes Italians when they are neither speaking nor singing, one will notice that they are not in the habit of clenching their teeth, as English-speaking persons tend to do. But, while their lips are closed, they relax and drop their lower jaw together with their tongue. The tongue lies on the floor of the mouth and is so relaxed and spread out that its front and sides are in contact with, and even slightly above, the lower teeth. This is the Italian basic tongue position.

As a result it is easy for the tongue to accomplish its articulatory movements farther forward in the mouth and with greater speed, since there is only a short distance to cover to reach the upper teeth or the hard palate.

To acquire correctly articulated and sharply enunciated Italian consonants, one will have to adopt this relaxed and forward Italian basic tongue position.

Consonants In Connected Speech

Italian speech sounds succeed each other in an energetic and vigorous manner; a vowel is prepared during, and possibly even at the beginning of, the articulation of the preceding consonant. This will avoid an on-glide and will thus preserve the correct monophthongal quality of the vowel.

Conversely, a consonant should never be prepared ahead of time. Only when the vowel is completed should the consonant be attacked, promptly and vigorously.

2 SINGLE AND DOUBLE CONSONANTS

OUTLINE

Unlike English, French and German, Italian differentiates consistently in speech and singing between the length of a single and of a double consonant.

For the articulation of Single Consonants, see Section (A).

For the articulation of Double Consonants, see Section (B).

For the special rules concerning the length of *r,* see Section 3(E) on the Dental *r*.

DISCUSSION

In English, double consonants do not stand for long consonants. There is no difference in length between the double *l* of *mellow* and the single *l* of *melon* or between the double *r* of *merry* and the single *r* of *very*.

In French (except in a few verb forms, and some learned bookish words or words of foreign origin), there is no difference between the length of a single and a double consonant.

Although in German lyric diction double consonants are prolonged, in conversation all consonants, whether single or double, are short.

In contrast to English, French and German, Italian distinguishes consistently between the length of a single and of a double consonant, in conversation as well as in lyric diction.

In Italian, a single consonant is short and is preceded by a long vowel; a double consonant is long and is preceded by a short vowel. And just as single and double consonants constantly alternate in spelling, so do short and long consonants in speaking and singing. This endows the Italian language with a peculiar vitality, a lilting cadence, which is one of its distinguishing features.

It is important that this characteristic be understood and respected, not only to preserve the peculiar lilt of the language, but also to avoid confusion. For in many instances a short single consonant with its long preceding vowel, and a long double consonant with its short preceding vowel, are the only means of distinguishing one word from another, as with *note* ['nɔtɛ] (*notes*) and *notte* ['nɔttɛ] (*night*), or *fumo* ['fumɔ] (*smoke*) and *fummo* ['fummɔ] (*we were*). More examples will be given later.

(A) Single Consonants

In Italian lyric diction a single consonant is short whether it is initial, between vowels, next to a consonant or final.

Initial Consonants

Initial consonants should be short even though uttered with the required energy and crispness.

Yet, when the initial consonant is a "continuant" (a consonant which may be sustained), such as *l, m, n* or *v,* English-speaking people tend to prolong it. Thus they prolong the initial *m* in *"Marcello, finalmente!"* [mɑr'tʃɛllɔ finɑl'mentɛ] in *La Bohème*, Act III or the initial *v* in *"Vissi d'arte, . . ."* ['vissi 'dɑrtɛ] in *Tosca,* Act II.

This lingering on an initial continuant, although a characteristic of English and other Germanic languages, does not apply to Italian.

EXERCISE

Speak, then sing, using a vigorous but short initial:

loco [ˈlɔkɔ]
lago [ˈlɑgɔ]
lento [ˈlɛntɔ]
mare [ˈmɑɾɛ]
mano [ˈmɑnɔ]
muto [ˈmutɔ]
nodo [ˈnɔdɔ]
nido [ˈnidɔ]

nave [ˈnɑvɛ]
vela [ˈvelɑ]
vita [ˈvitɑ]
vero [ˈveɾɔ]
livido [ˈlividɔ]
lontano [lɔnˈtɑnɔ]
lampada [ˈlɑmpɑdɑ]
malore [mɑˈloɾɛ]

medico [ˈmɛdikɔ]
musica [ˈmuzikɑ]
nuvola [ˈnuvɔlɑ]
nemico [nɛˈmikɔ]
natura [nɑˈtuɾɑ]
vergine [ˈverdʒinɛ]
veloce [vɛˈlotʃɛ]
verbena [vɛrˈbɛnɑ]

Single Consonants Between Vowels

A single consonant between vowels, though brisk and energetic, should be particularly short, and the vowel preceding it should be distinctly lengthened.

Each of the words *amo* [ˈɑmɔ], *odo* [ˈɔdɔ], *eco* [ˈɛkɔ], *ira* [ˈiɾɑ] has a long initial vowel and a clean-cut, curt consonant.

Such a consonant should be so short as to give the illusion that the two vowels adjoin—that is, that the vowel line is not interrupted. To illustrate this point graphically, the word *amo* should be spelled *aaaaaaa-moooooooo*.

SYLLABIFICATION

Syllabically, a single consonant between vowels belongs to the vowel that follows, never to the preceding one. It should be spoken as the beginning of the second syllable and should be sung on the pitch of the second vowel.

The correct syllabification of the following is *pa-ro-la* [pɑ-ˈɾɔ-lɑ] not *par-ol-a, a-mo-re* [ɑ-ˈmo-ɾɛ] not *am-or-e, fa-ta-le* [fɑ-ˈtɑ-lɛ] not *fat-al-e*.

To overcome the widespread habit among English-speaking singers of anticipating single consonants between vowels and holding them instead of holding the preceding vowel, one should concentrate on sustaining the vowel until it is time for the consonant to begin the following syllable and note. The resulting prolonged monophthongs are one of the characteristics of Italian. They are as essential in singing Italian as they are beneficial to singing in general, since it is the vowel which carries the tone.

EXERCISE I

In speaking, then singing, the following words, first eliminate the medial consonant, while sounding prolonged contiguous vowels with a legato. Later, add the medial consonant, making sure that it be short enough not to interfere with the continuity of the vowel line. Thinking of singing through each consonant, even if it is a voiceless one, will help preserve the integrity of such a vowel line.

tela ['tela]	nome ['nomɛ]	vino ['vinɔ]
stelo ['stɛlɔ]	come ['komɛ]	tana ['tana]
fole ['fɔlɛ]	nume ['numɛ]	seta ['seta]
male ['malɛ]	dama ['dama]	fato ['fatɔ]
ala ['ala]	uomo ['wɔmɔ]	gote ['gɔtɛ]
mela ['mela]	cane ['kanɛ]	cupo ['kupɔ]
sole ['solɛ]	dono ['donɔ]	stipo ['stipɔ]
gola ['gola]	bene ['bɛnɛ]	capo ['kapɔ]
lume ['lumɛ]	lana ['lana]	avi ['avi]
fumo ['fumɔ]	luna ['luna]	neve ['nevɛ]
fama ['fama]	cena ['tʃena]	

EXERCISE II

Apply the same technique with the following words.

amami ['amami]	nemico [nɛ'mikɔ]
idolo ['idɔlɔ]	povera ['pɔvɛɾa]
parola [pa'ɾɔla]	amabile [a'mabilɛ]
dolore [dɔ'loɾɛ]	benevolo [bɛ'nɛvɔlɔ]
fedele [fɛ'dɛlɛ]	malevolo [ma'lɛvɔlɔ]
nobile ['nɔbilɛ]	fatalità [fatali'ta]
baleno [ba'lenɔ]	sciagurato [ʃagu'ɾatɔ]
malore [ma'loɾɛ]	avevamo [avɛ'vamɔ]
felice [fɛ'litʃɛ]	favorevole [favɔ'ɾevɔlɛ]

Single Consonants Followed By Other Consonants

In lyric diction a single consonant followed by one or two other consonants is short and it is the preceding vowel which is long.

Even though an *l, m* or *n* followed by one or two other consonants (as in *altro* ['altrɔ], *sempre* ['sɛmprɛ]) belongs to the first syllable and the following consonant or consonants belong to the second syllable, nevertheless the *l, m* or *n* is short and should be spoken at the very end of the first syllable, following a long vowel.

The adjoining consonants must be in perfect contact with each other. No neutral vowel [ə] should be interpolated. Some singers have this habit which stems from eagerness to enunciate every consonant distinctly. But this results in a distortion of words and phrases which renders the text unintelligible.

Consonants should be enunciated with care but they must combine and blend with one another smoothly, effortlessly and without intrusive vowel sounds.

Canto is pronounced ['kantɔ], not ['kanətɔ].

EXERCISE

Speak, then sing, the following with sustained vowels, first without and later with, the consonants.

caldo ['kɑldɔ]	vampa ['vɑmpɑ]	canto ['kɑntɔ]
alba ['ɑlbɑ]	bimba ['bimbɑ]	landa ['lɑndɑ]
molto ['moltɔ]	ombra ['ombrɑ]	fonte ['fontɛ]
stolto ['stoltɔ]	tomba ['tombɑ]	monti ['monti]
altro ['ɑltrɔ]	empio ['empjɔ]	danza ['dɑntsɑ]
alto ['ɑltɔ]	scempio ['ʃempjɔ]	antro ['ɑntrɔ]
falso ['fɑlsɔ]	tempre ['tɛmprɛ]	contro ['kontrɔ]
scaltro ['skɑltrɔ]	strambo ['strɑmbɔ]	stanza ['stɑntsɑ]
fulcro ['fulkrɔ]	sempre ['sɛmprɛ]	scontro ['skontrɔ]

Final Consonants

Except for the final *d* in the monosyllables *ed* ['ed], *ad* ['ɑd] and *od* ['od] (sometimes used in front of a vowel for *e* ['e], *a* ['ɑ] and *o* ['o]), the only consonants which may be final in Italian are *l, m, n* and *r*. Thus we have *fedel* [fɛ'dɛl], *andiam* [ɑn'djɑm], *buon* ['bwɔn], *amor* [ɑ'mor].

Although the final *r* should be prolonged and rolled, the final *l, m* or *n* is short and preceded by a long vowel.

This may present some difficulty to English-speaking singers who tend to anticipate and prolong the final consonant at the expense of the length of the preceding vowel.

That the preceding vowel must be long is evidenced by the fact that, should the consonant-final be followed by a vowel-initial within the phrase, the consonant-final will have to be sung with this vowel-initial and on its pitch. As a result, the preceding vowel will last the whole length of the note value.

More will be said about this in Part VII which deals with WORDS IN CONTEXT (See Section 3(C)).

EXERCISE

Speak, then sing, the following prolonging the last vowel and articulating a short, sharp final consonant.

il ['il]	uom ['wɔm]	in ['in]
del ['dɛl]	siam ['sjɑm]	son ['son]
bel ['bɛl]	vediam [vɛ'djɑm]	sen ['sen]
sol ['sol]	andiam [ɑn'djɑm]	man ['mɑn]
esil ['ɛzil]	godiam [gɔ'djɑm]	velen [vɛ'len]
fatal [fɑ'tɑl]	beviam [bɛ'vjɑm]	ruban ['rubɑn]
natal [nɑ'tɑl]	fuggiam [fud'dʒɑm]	invan [in'vɑn]
amabil [ɑ'mɑbil]	lavoriam [lɑvɔ'ɾjɑm]	almen [ɑl'men]

(B) Double Consonants

A double consonant maintains all the acoustic characteristics of the single consonant, except for its length, which is many times that of a single consonant. The time required for the lengthening of the double consonant is taken from the preceding vowel, which is distinctly shortened.

For instance, each of the words *ella* ['ellɑ], *inno* ['innɔ], *otto* ['ɔttɔ], *ecco* ['ɛkkɔ] has a very short initial vowel and a long double consonant.

SYLLABIFICATION

The first consonant of a double consonant belongs syllabically to the preceding vowel and must be sung on its pitch. The second consonant belongs to the following vowel and its pitch. In other words, the consonants belong to two different syllables and notes and must be sung accordingly but without a break.

DIRECTIONS

To sing a double consonant one will have to begin it at the end of the first syllable and note and to hold it through the beginning of the second syllable and note without shifting the position of the speech organs. The beginning of the second syllable and note will require a slight breath impulse—that is, a somewhat intensified flow of breath.

LENGTH OF DOUBLE CONSONANTS

The question arises as to how long a double consonant should be held. It would be helpful if one could state exactly how many times longer than a single consonant a double consonant should be. But this is impossible in singing where the duration of speech sounds is influenced not only by the tempo of the music but also by the rhythmic pattern underlying each phrase. Nevertheless the following point should be made.

Although the length of the preceding vowel and the shortness of the single consonant and the shortness of the preceding vowel and the length of the double consonant depend on tempo and rhythm, nevertheless there must be a distinct, unmistakable difference between the length of the vowel and the consonant, no matter how fast or slow the tempo is, or how short or long the note. Otherwise what is sung would not be Italian.

The following will clarify this point. Since there are no syllabic consonants in Italian (see Part VI on SYLLABIFICATION), a vowel must be part of every syllable. Consequently, when singing double consonants every note and every beat must include a vowel.

For example, in Amneris' outcry in the first act of *Aida*

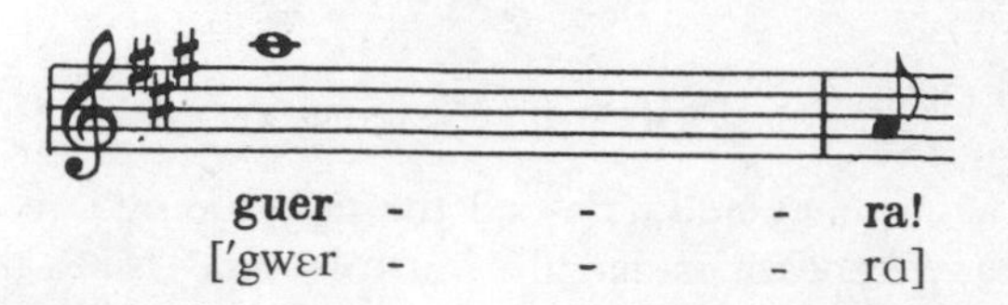

the stressed vowel [ɛ] must be held through the first three beats of the measure and through the beginning of the fourth beat. Only then should the rolled *r* be started. The correct way to sing this could be expressed as *gueeee-eeee-eeee-eeerr-rraaaa*. The young aspiring Amneris who once attempted to sing it as *gueerr-rrrr-rrrr-rrrr-rraa* interrupted herself with a burst of laughter, for she realized how unmusical it sounded.

Before concluding, for those who want a practical guide as to the length of double consonants we say (although well aware of the limitations of such a statement): a double consonant should never be shorter than four times the duration of a single consonant.

Single And Double Consonants Compared

Following is a list of words whose meaning changes with the doubling of one consonant.

Study it, then speak and sing the words going across from left to right. It is important to repractice them after you know more about the pronunciation of Italian consonants.

SINGLE CONSONANT WORDS	DOUBLE CONSONANT WORDS
CONSONANT: short,	long.
PRECEDING VOWEL: long,	short.
VOWEL LINE: uninterrupted,	interrupted by long consonant.
SYLLABICATION: consonant spoken and sung with and on pitch of following vowel,	first consonant spoken and sung with preceding vowel, second with following vowel.
anelo [ɑ'nɛlɔ] *I long*	anello [ɑ'nɛllɔ] *ring* (n.)
aprendo [ɑ'prɛndɔ] *opening* (gerund)	apprendo [ɑp'prɛndɔ] *I learn*
aringa [ɑ'ɾiŋgɑ] *herring*	arringa [ɑr'riŋgɑ] *harangue*
bela ['bɛlɑ] *it bleats*	bella ['bɛllɑ] *beautiful*
bruto ['brutɔ] *brute*	brutto ['bruttɔ] *ugly*
camino [kɑ'minɔ] *chimney*	cammino [kɑm'minɔ] *road, way*
cane ['kɑnɛ] *dog*	canne ['kɑnnɛ] *reeds*
caro ['kɑɾɔ] *dear*	carro ['kɑrrɔ] *cart* (n.)
eco ['ɛkɔ] *echo*	ecco ['ɛkkɔ] *here is,* etc.
ero ['ɛɾɔ] *I was*	erro ['ɛrrɔ] *I err*
face ['fɑtʃɛ] *torch, light*	facce ['fɑttʃɛ] *faces* (n.)
fato ['fɑtɔ] *fate*	fatto ['fɑttɔ] *done*
fero ['fɛɾɔ] *proud, cruel*	ferro ['fɛrrɔ] *iron* (n.)

fioco ['fjɔkɔ] *feeble*	fiocco ['fjɔkkɔ] *bow, tassel*
fola ['fɔlɑ] *story, tale*	folla ['fɔllɑ] *crowd* (n.)
fumo ['fumɔ] *smoke* (n.)	fummo ['fummɔ] *we were*
gema ['dʒɛmɑ] *let him moan*	gemma ['dʒɛmmɑ] *gem*
invito [in'vitɔ] *invitation*	invitto [in'vittɔ] *unvanquished*
mole ['mɔlɛ] *bulk*	molle ['mɔllɛ] *soft*
moto ['mɔtɔ] *motion*	motto ['mɔttɔ] *slogan*
nono ['nɔnɔ] *ninth*	nonno ['nɔnnɔ] *grandfather*
note ['nɔtɛ] *notes* (n.)	notte ['nɔttɛ] *night*
pani ['pɑni] *loaves, breads*	panni ['pɑnni] *clothes*
pena ['penɑ] *pain*	penna ['pennɑ] *pen, feather*
rida ['ridɑ] *may he laugh*	ridda ['riddɑ] *confusion*
rupe ['rupɛ] *rock* (n.)	ruppe ['ruppɛ] *he broke*
seno ['senɔ] *bosom*	senno ['sennɔ] *wisdom*
sono ['sonɔ] *I am, they are*	sonno ['sonnɔ] *sleep* (n.)
stile ['stilɛ] *style*	stille ['stillɛ] *drops* (n.)
vano ['vɑnɔ] *vain*	vanno ['vɑnnɔ] *they go*
vendete [vɛn'detɛ] *you sell*	vendette [vɛn'dettɛ] *revenge*
vile ['vilɛ] *coward*	ville ['villɛ] *country houses*

Two Double Consonants Within A Word

Two double consonants within one word occur fairly frequently in Italian. Examples are the endearing *Susannetta* [suzɑn'nettɑ] with which Cherubino addresses Susanna in *Le nozze di Figaro* or *Nannetta* [nɑn'nettɑ] in *Falstaff* or the words *donnetta* [dɔn'nettɑ], *cappello* [kɑp'pɛllɔ] and *parrucca* [pɑr'rukkɑ].

To a non-native (or to an Italian with the regional habit of not lengthening double consonants), it may seem difficult to sing a sequence of doubles. However, it pertains to the language and it is a skill actually not difficult to acquire. The important point to remember is to shorten the preceding vowels sufficiently so as to have the time required for the lengthening of the consonants themselves.

When two doubled consonants follow each other the tendency is to ignore the lengthening of the first double consonant and to concentrate on doubling only the second. *Nannetta* [nɑn'nettɑ] will then sound like *Nanetta* [nɑ'nettɑ] and *parrucca* [pɑr'rukkɑ] like *parucca* [pɑ'rukkɑ]. Obviously this is not correct. Both doubles must be lengthened. It will therefore be helpful to concentrate particularly on the first double consonant, shortening its preceding vowel energetically and lengthening the consonant itself.

EXERCISE

Speak, then sing:

affetto [ɑf'fɛttɔ]	affanni [ɑf'fɑnni]
afflitto [ɑf'flittɔ]	affitto [ɑf'fittɔ]

uccelli [ut'tʃɛlli]
addosso [ɑd'dɔssɔ]
gonnella [gɔn'nɛllɑ]
abbraccio [ɑb'brɑttʃɔ]
carrozza [kɑr'rɔttsɑ]
accoppio [ɑk'kɔppjɔ]
oppresso [ɔp'prɛssɔ]
appellano [ɑp'pɛllɑnɔ]
pennacchini [pɛnnɑk'kini]
zeffiretti [dzɛffi'ɾetti]

ballatella [bɑllɑ'tɛllɑ]
farfalletta [fɑrfɑl'lettɑ]
folleggiare [fɔllɛd'dʒɑɾɛ]
inneggiamo [innɛd'dʒɑmɔ]
trabocchetto [trɑbɔk'kettɔ]
appassionata [ɑppɑssjɔ'nɑtɑ]
esterrefatta [ɛstɛrrɛ'fɑttɑ]
Nannetta [nɑn'nettɑ]
Fiammetta [fjɑm'mettɑ]
Susannetta [suzɑn'nettɑ]

Italian Double Consonants Compared To French And German Ones

As stated before, Italian double consonants are long, and they shorten their preceding vowels.

On the other hand, French and German double consonants, which are lengthened only occasionally, influence the sound character of the preceding vowel. The first vowel of the French words *belle, terre, homme, botte* and of the German *Welle, essen, Sonne, kommen* are all open (pronounced [ɛ] or [ɔ]), because they precede a double consonant.

This does not apply to Italian where a double consonant influences only the length and not the sound of the preceding vowel. Only in Italian, therefore, may an open as well as a close vowel precede a double consonant, as in *legge* ['leddʒɛ] (*law*) and *legge* ['lɛddʒɛ] (*he reads*), *botte* ['bottɛ] (*barrel*) and *botte* ['bɔttɛ] (*blows,* n.), etc.

Vowel Length In Italian Lyric Diction

As a result of the discussion of the length of single and double consonants as related to the length of the preceding vowel, the following important rule is given.

RULE

In Italian lyric diction all vowels are long except the ones preceding a double consonant.

3 THE DENTAL CONSONANTS *l, n, d, t, r*

OUTLINE

Unlike English, the Italian consonants *l, n, d, t* and *r* are dental.

For the Dental *l,* see Section (A).

For the Dental *n,* see Section (B).

For the Dental *d,* see Section (C). Since the Italian *d* is Fully Voiced, see also Section 5(B).

For the Dental *t*, see Section (D). Since the Italian *t* is Unaspirated, see also Section 4(B).

For the Dental *r*, see Section (E).

To remember which consonants are dental in Italian, think of the words *linden tree* which include them all.

The Dentals And Exercising The Tongue

The English consonants *l, n, d, t* and *r* are "alveolar" or "gum ridge" consonants since they are produced with the tip of the tongue either on or near the upper gum ridge. Their Italian counterparts are "dental" because they are articulated with the tip of the tongue directly touching the inner surface of the upper front teeth.

As long as the touching of the teeth requires a motion smaller than that of reaching for the gum ridge, the Italian dentals allow for, and require, an increased relaxation of the rest of the tongue, and of the jaw and throat as well. This in turn facilitates the correct monophthongal production of the vowel preceding the dental.

Because they are produced farther forward in the mouth, these Italian consonants will also sound farther forward and will have a more penetrating character than the English sounds. Their correct production will greatly contribute to the intelligibility of the text.

Also, since one of the functions of the consonant is to release and give impulse to the vowel that follows, and since it is the vowel that carries the tone, the dental *l, n, d, t* and *r* will indirectly enhance the resonating and carrying power of the voice itself.

Thus few tongue exercises will contribute more toward the control of jaw and tongue as well as toward the physiological freedom of the voice than prolonged work on the five Italian dentals.

REMARK

French, Spanish, Latin and German use dental consonants too.

(A) The Dental *l*

CLASSIFICATION

The Italian *l* is a "dental voiced lateral" consonant (see Chart I).

DISCUSSION

Unlike the English alveolar *l*, the Italian *l* is "dental," made with the tip of the tongue lightly touching the inside of the upper incisors. The difference in sound is striking, as the dental *l* sounds farther forward, clearer and sharper than the alveolar one.

The *l* is further classified as "lateral" to indicate that while the tip of the tongue is in contact with the upper teeth the breath escapes laterally over the sides of the tongue.

Finally, the Italian *l* is a fully "voiced" consonant—that is, it is accompanied by vibrations of the vocal cords throughout.

REMARK

A prerequisite for the correct dentalization of the Italian *l* is a complete relaxation of jaw and tongue. One must avoid not only muscular involvement of the jaw—which should remain limp and inactive—but also any tensing, thickening or backing of the tongue which would result in throatiness. The articulatory movement is made neither by the jaw nor by the bulk of the tongue, but only by the tip of the tongue.

Practicing Dental Single *l*

A single *l* is very short no matter what its position in the word.

EXERCISE I: Initial *l* and Single *l* between Vowels

Speak, then sing, using a short dental *l:*

[liiiiliiiiliiii] [luuuuluuuuluuuu]
[leeeeleeeeleeee] [looooloooolooooo]
[lɛɛɛɛlɛɛɛɛlɛɛɛɛ] [lɔɔɔɔlɔɔɔɔlɔɔɔɔ]
[lɑɑɑɑlɑɑɑɑlɑɑɑɑ]

Align your body, use a mirror, speak up and listen carefully to yourself.

At the start of each exercise let your jaw fall silently open through its own weight by simply relaxing it. The tongue which will be in its basic position will fall with the jaw by its own weight. From this position the short *l* is produced by swiftly raising the tip of the tongue to the inside of the upper teeth and swiftly letting it fall back to its basic position to start the vowel.

The jaw should remain open and motionless in an effortless, relaxed fashion throughout.

Even before the initial *l* is started the lips should be shaped in the position of the vowel. They should be soft and relaxed and should maintain their shape until the exercise is completed, and even an instant beyond, so as to avoid off-glides.

The initial *l* is short, much shorter than an English initial *l*. Since the second and third *l*'s are single between vowels, they are also extremely short and must be preceded by a long vowel. Syllabically, these *l*'s belong to the vowel that follows.

Therefore this is an exercise with three very short *l*'s and three prolonged vowels. The vowels should be so long and the *l*'s should require a movement of the tip of the tongue so rapid and limited in its span as to give the illusion of hearing one single uninterrupted long vowel. But this is only an illusion since the *l*'s, no matter how short, should be uttered vigorously and distinctly.

To acquire the required long vowels and short single consonants, first practice this exercise with its long vowels only. It would then sound like an uninterrupted, long *iiiiiiiiiii*. If you use a well-supported voice, sustained vowels and a perfect legato, you will be able to add the missing *l*'s later without giving up the long, almost uninterrupted vowel line.

EXERCISE II: Final *l*

Speak, then sing, using a short dental *l:*

[iiiiiiiil] [uuuuuuuul]
[eeeeeeeel] [oooooooool]
[ɛɛɛɛɛɛɛɛl] [ɔɔɔɔɔɔɔɔl]
[ɑɑɑɑɑɑɑɑl]

The jaw should fall open through its own weight and the tongue, resting on the floor of the mouth, should drop with the jaw. The lips should assume the formation required by the vowel before the vowel is started. They should maintain this formation until the articulation of the short final *l* is completed, and even an instant beyond.

The jaw should not move during the entire exercise and the tongue should remain relaxed and inactive except for the tip, which does the articulatory movement so swiftly and lightly as to barely make contact with the teeth.

REMARK

It is particularly an *l* final in word or syllable that English-speaking persons have difficulty dentalizing. They may use the ample and slow tongue movement characteristic of the alveolar *l*, which unduly lengthens the *l*. They tend to anticipate the *l* instead of giving almost the whole length of the note value to the preceding vowel. They tend to thicken and darken a final *l* into a throaty consonant, which results from muscular tension in the tongue. They tend also to diphthongize the preceding vowel by adding the neutral vowel [ə] before the *l* is sounded.

Follow all directions carefully, and the final *l* will sound as clear, precise, short and genuinely dental as it should.

EXERCISE III: Single *l* Words

Speak, then sing, concentrating on a dental and short single *l:*

(a) INITIAL *l*

luce ['lutʃɛ]	lume ['lumɛ]	lusinghiero [luziŋ'gjɛɾɔ]
luna ['luna]	lagrima ['lagrima]	Liù ['lju]
lesto ['lɛstɔ]	leggero [lɛd'dʒɛɾɔ]	Laura ['laːŭɾa]
larva ['larva]	lucente [lu'tʃɛntɛ]	Lucia [lu'tʃiːa]
labbro ['labbrɔ]	lealtà [lɛal'ta]	Luigi [lu'idʒi]
latte ['lattɛ]	lettore [lɛt'toɾɛ]	Lindoro [lin'dɔɾɔ]
landa ['landa]	libertà [libɛr'ta]	Lodovico [lɔdɔ'vikɔ]
lode ['lɔdɛ]	lacerato [latʃɛ'ɾatɔ]	Leonora [lɛɔ'nɔɾa]

(b) SINGLE *l* BETWEEN VOWELS

gelo ['dʒɛlɔ]	gelosia [dʒɛlɔ'ziːa]
cielo ['tʃɛlɔ]	naturale [natu'ɾalɛ]
miele ['mjɛlɛ]	cavaliere [kava'ljɛɾɛ]
bile ['bilɛ]	maledetto [malɛ'dettɔ]
vile ['vilɛ]	galantuomo [galanˌtwɔmɔ]
gala ['gala]	celestiale [tʃɛlɛ'stjalɛ]
vela ['vela]	Lola ['lɔla]
malia [ma'liːa]	Bartolo ['bartɔlɔ]
fatale [fa'talɛ]	Eleonora [ɛlɛɔ'nɔɾa]
crudele [kru'dɛlɛ]	Don Pasquale ['dɔn pa'skwalɛ]
salute [sa'lutɛ]	Malatesta [mala'tɛsta]

(c) FINAL *l*

quel ['kwel]	crudel [kru'dɛl]	natural [natu'ɾal]
dal ['dal]	augel [aːŭ'dʒɛl]	celestial [tʃɛlɛ'stjal]
mal ['mal]	gioiel [dʒɔ'jɛl]	imperial [impɛ'ɾjal]
suol ['swɔl]	anel [a'nɛl]	giovanil [dʒɔva'nil]
duol ['dwɔl]	regal [rɛ'gal]	implacabil [impla'kabil]
col ['kɔl]	nobil ['nɔbil]	Natal [na'tal]
sul ['sul]	facil ['fatʃil]	Parpignol [parpi'ɲɔl]
fedel [fɛ'dɛl]	terribil [tɛr'ribil]	Fanuel [fanu'ɛl]

(d) *l* NEXT TO A CONSONANT

The following are words in which a single *l* either precedes or follows another consonant.

In words in which it precedes the consonant, the *l* should be neither anticipated nor sustained.

In addition, an *l* should be in perfect contact with the neighboring consonant. No neutral vowel [ə] should intrude. The word is *alma* ['alma], not ['aləma]; *plauso* ['plaːŭzɔ], not [pə'laːŭzɔ].

Speak and then sing:

salce ['saltʃɛ]	alfine [al'finɛ]	malvagio [mal'vadʒɔ]
falco ['falkɔ]	sleale [zlɛ'alɛ]	soldato [sɔl'datɔ]
dolce ['doltʃɛ]	malcauto [mal'ka:ŭtɔ]	Silvio ['silvjɔ]
scaltro ['skaltrɔ]	altrove [al'trovɛ]	Alfio ['alfjɔ]
plauso ['pla:ŭzɔ]	afflitto [af'flittɔ]	Gilda ['dʒilda]
flauto ['fla:ŭtɔ]	silfidi ['silfidi]	Florindo [flɔ'ɾindɔ]
slaccia ['zlattʃa]	placido ['platʃidɔ]	Ulrica [ul'rika]
oblio [ɔ'bli:ɔ]	effluvio [ɛf'fluvjɔ]	Alcindoro [altʃin'dɔɾɔ]

PRACTICING DENTAL DOUBLE *l*

Since a double consonant maintains all the acoustic characteristics of the single consonant, a double *l* will be as dental as a single one. Although the tip of the tongue must rest on the teeth for a longer period of time the jaw and tongue should not be tense, for this would bring about a throaty quality. Articulating a double *l* is not a matter of increased effort but of correct timing. The preceding vowel should be vigorously shortened, and if only the tip of the tongue is active and rests gently against the upper teeth for the required length of time, an effortless, clear and resonant dental double *l* will result.

The preceding vowel should be short, but not choked so as to lose its acoustic characteristics.

Syllabically a double *l* belongs to two different vowels, syllables and notes. The word *bella* ['bɛlla], for instance, does not contain just a lengthened *l;* it consists of the syllable *bel,* which has a final *l,* and of the syllable *la* which has an initial *l.* Though the two *l*'s are uttered without a break, the second *l* should begin with a slight breath impulse of its own.

EXERCISE

Speak, then sing:

fallo ['fallɔ]	anello [a'nɛllɔ]	agnellina [aɲɛl'lina]
stella ['stella]	augello [a:ŭ'dʒɛllɔ]	Ballo ['ballɔ]
spalla ['spalla]	fellone [fɛl'lonɛ]	Otello [ɔ'tɛllɔ]
folla ['fɔlla]	valloni [val'loni]	Fiorello [fjɔ'ɾɛllɔ]
colle ['kɔllɛ]	sigillo [si'dʒillɔ]	Marcello [mar'tʃɛllɔ]
nulla ['nulla]	follia [fɔl'li:a]	Dorabella [dɔɾa'bɛlla]
ella ['ella]	collina [kɔl'lina]	Leporello [lɛpɔ'ɾɛllɔ]
quello ['kwellɔ]	farfallone [farfal'lonɛ]	Cavalleria [kavallɛ'ɾi:a]

(B) THE DENTAL *n*

CLASSIFICATION

The Italian *n* is a "dental voiced nasal" consonant (see Chart I).

DISCUSSION

Unlike the English alveolar *n,* the Italian *n* is "dental," made by lightly touching the inside of the upper teeth with the tip of the tongue. As a result it sounds farther forward and clearer than the English *n.*

The *n* is further classified as "nasal," to indicate that the breath escapes through the nose. Also, the *n* is a "voiced" consonant.

Thus, the Italian *l* and *n* are both dental and voiced. In addition they both belong to the consonants called "continuants" (consonants which can be prolonged, see Chart I). The only difference between *l* and *n* lies in the manner of articulation since the *l* is a lateral and the *n* is a nasal.

REMARK

Because of the shared characteristics of the Italian *l* and *n,* the directions given for dental *l* are just as valid for dental *n.*

To avoid repetition, we will refer to the suggestions outlined in the preceding section on the Dental *l.*

PRACTICING DENTAL SINGLE *n*

A single *n* is very short, no matter what its position in the word.

EXERCISE I: Initial *n* and Single *n* between Vowels

Speak, then sing, using a very short dental *n:*

[niiiiniiiiniiii] [nuuuunuuuunuuuu]
[neeeeneeeeneeee] [noooonoooonoooo]
[nɛɛɛɛnɛɛɛɛnɛɛɛɛ] [nɔɔɔɔnɔɔɔɔnɔɔɔɔ]
[nɑɑɑɑnɑɑɑɑnɑɑɑɑ]

Refer to the Directions in Section (A), Exercise I.

EXERCISE II: Final *n*

Speak, then sing, using a short dental *n:*

[iiiiiiiin] [uuuuuuuun]
[eeeeeeeen] [oooooooon]
[ɛɛɛɛɛɛɛɛn] [ɔɔɔɔɔɔɔɔn]
[ɑɑɑɑɑɑɑɑn]

Refer to the Directions in Section (A), Exercise II.

EXERCISE III: Single *n* Words

Speak, then sing, using a short dental *n:*

(a) INITIAL *n*

no ['nɔ]	nulla ['nullɑ]	nessuno [nɛs'sunɔ]
nome ['nomɛ]	natura [nɑ'turɑ]	notaio [nɔ'tɑjɔ]
neve ['nevɛ]	narrare [nɑr'rɑrɛ]	novità [nɔvi'tɑ]
nero ['nerɔ]	nuvole ['nuvɔlɛ]	neppure [nɛp'purɛ]
naso ['nɑzɔ]	nobile ['nɔbilɛ]	Nina ['ninɑ]
nebbie ['nebbjɛ]	nemico [nɛ'mikɔ]	Nilo ['nilɔ]
netto ['nettɔ]	nascosta [nɑ'skostɑ]	Nerone [nɛ'ronɛ]
nodo ['nɔdɔ]	notturno [nɔt'turnɔ]	Norina [nɔ'rinɑ]

(b) SINGLE *n* BETWEEN VOWELS

mano ['mɑnɔ]	anima ['ɑnimɑ]	onore [ɔ'norɛ]
buono ['bwɔnɔ]	anello [ɑ'nɛllɔ]	Tonio ['tɔnjɔ]
sono ['sonɔ]	piccina [pit'tʃinɑ]	Renato [rɛ'nɑtɔ]
uno ['unɔ]	collina [kɔl'linɑ]	Zerlina [dzɛr'linɑ]
pena ['penɑ]	venire [vɛ'nirɛ]	Rosina [rɔ'zinɑ]
strano ['strɑnɔ]	barone [bɑ'ronɛ]	Elena ['ɛlɛnɑ]
pane ['pɑnɛ]	verbena [vɛr'bɛnɑ]	Fenena [fɛ'nɛnɑ]
vano ['vɑnɔ]	manina [mɑ'ninɑ]	Leonora [lɛɔ'nɔrɑ]

(c) FINAL *n*

dan ['dɑn]	gran ['grɑn]	vedon ['vedɔn]
stan ['stɑn]	ben ['bɛn]	giuran ['dʒurɑn]
fan ['fɑn]	mattin [mɑt'tin]	capitan ['kɑpitɑn]
van ['vɑn]	fellon [fɛl'lon]	bevon ['bevɔn]
un ['un]	buffon [buf'fon]	poltron [pɔl'tron]
don ['don]	lontan [lɔn'tɑn]	pancion [pɑn'tʃon]
don ['dɔn]	cantan ['kɑntɑn]	Simon [si'mon]
buon ['bwɔn]	danzan ['dɑntsɑn]	Cherubin [kɛru'bin]

(d) *n* NEXT TO A CONSONANT

Refer to the Directions in Section (A), Exercise III (d).

vanto ['vɑntɔ]	tanfo ['tɑnfɔ]	speranza [spɛ'rɑntsɑ]
manto ['mɑntɔ]	ventura [vɛn'turɑ]	snudare [znu'dɑrɛ]
tondo ['tondɔ]	sventura [zvɛn'turɑ]	fanciulla [fɑn'tʃullɑ]
mondo ['mondɔ]	piangere ['pjɑndʒɛrɛ]	Arno ['ɑrnɔ]
gente ['dʒɛntɛ]	governo [gɔ'vɛrnɔ]	Santa ['sɑntɑ]
snello ['znɛllɔ]	eterno [ɛ'tɛrnɔ]	Ernani [ɛr'nɑni]
ninfa ['ninfɑ]	indarno [in'dɑrnɔ]	Gioconda [dʒɔ'kondɑ]
senza ['sɛntsɑ]	malnato [mɑl'nɑtɔ]	Cenerentola [tʃɛnɛ'rɛntɔlɑ]

EXERCISE IV: *n* Followed by [k] or [g]

In conversational Italian, an *n* followed by either [k] or [g] is not dental but "mediopalatal." It sounds like the final consonant in the English *sing, long* (IPA symbol [ŋ]). But there is a difference between the English and the Italian [ŋ]; in Italian it is articulated with the center of the tongue against the junction of the hard and soft palates, not against the soft palate as in English. Thus, the Italian [ŋ] is produced farther forward.

In Italian lyric diction, however, the often-heard dental *n* substituting for the mediopalatal [ŋ] before [k] or [g] is permissible, since the dental *n* is produced still farther forward in the mouth and is more resonant.

If the dental *n* is used, care must be taken that it be in perfect contact with the following [k] or [g] and that no neutral vowel intrude between the two. For instance, the word *sangue* is pronounced ['sɑngwɛ], not ['sɑnəgwɛ].

Since the [ŋ] and the [n] are both permissible in this particular position, for example: ['fɑŋgɔ] as well as ['fɑngɔ], practice the following words, using both sounds alternately.

stanco ['stɑŋkɔ] and ['stɑnkɔ]
sangue ['sɑŋgwɛ] and ['sɑngwɛ]
bianca ['bjɑŋkɑ], etc.
vengo ['vɛŋgɔ]
tengo ['tɛŋgɔ]
manco ['mɑŋkɔ]
dunque ['duŋkwɛ]
fingo ['fiŋgɔ]
lungo ['luŋgɔ]
anche ['ɑŋkɛ]
finchè [fiŋ'ke]
benchè [bɛŋ'ke]
fandango [fɑn'dɑŋgɔ]
languore [lɑŋ'gworɛ]
ancora ['ɑŋkɔrɑ]
ancora [ɑŋ'korɑ]
moncherino [mɔŋkɛ'rinɔ]
illanguidita [illɑŋgwi'ditɑ]
mancomale [mɑŋkɔ'mɑlɛ]
tranquilla [trɑŋ'kwillɑ]
tanghero ['tɑŋgɛrɔ]
Tinca ['tiŋkɑ]
Banco ['bɑŋkɔ]

When you feel secure in both techniques you may decide for yourself which of the two sounds suits you better, the [ŋ] or the [n].

PRACTICING DENTAL DOUBLE *n*

Refer to the Directions on Double *l*.

EXERCISE

anno ['ɑnnɔ]
inno ['innɔ]
donna ['dɔnnɑ]
danno ['dɑnnɔ]
gonna ['gɔnnɑ]
stanno ['stɑnnɔ]
vanno ['vɑnnɔ]
malanno [mɑ'lɑnnɔ]
affanno [ɑf'fɑnnɔ]
cannone [kɑn'nonɛ]
innanzi [in'nɑntsi]
annata [ɑn'nɑtɑ]
dannato [dɑn'nɑtɔ]
donnesco [dɔn'neskɔ]
rinnegata [rinnɛ'gɑtɑ]
innocente [innɔ'tʃɛntɛ]
fannullone [fɑnnul'lonɛ]
Gianni ['dʒɑnni]

Giovanni [dʒɔ'vɑnni] Nannetta [nɑn'nettɑ] Annina [ɑn'ninɑ]
Susanna [su'zɑnnɑ] Madonna [mɑ'dɔnnɑ] Sonnambula [sɔn'nɑmbulɑ]

(C) The Dental *d*

CLASSIFICATION

The Italian *d* is a "dental voiced plosive" consonant (see Chart I).

DISCUSSION

Unlike the English alveolar *d,* the Italian *d* is "dental," made with the tip of the tongue lightly touching the inside of the upper front teeth. It is produced farther forward in the mouth than the English *d.*

The *d* is further classified as a "voiced plosive." A plosive is a consonant characterized by a stoppage of the flow of breath (in the *d,* through the tip of the tongue against the upper teeth), followed by a sudden explosive release of the breath.

The English *d* is also a voiced plosive but in English speech the voicing of the *d* may be either complete or partial or even omitted, depending upon its position in the word and phrase and upon the speech characteristics of the speaker (see Part III, Section 5(B)).

In Italian, the *d* is invariably "fully voiced throughout"—the vocal cords vibrate and a pitch is audible through its articulation.

REMARK

As a plosive, the dental *d* requires a more complex action of the tip of the tongue than the continuants *l* and *n.* For the tip of the tongue must first stop the flow of breath through firm contact with the upper teeth and must hold the breath for an instant. Then it must suddenly release the breath by being abruptly flipped down to rest against the lower teeth.

This more complex tongue action still does not justify any tension. A completely relaxed jaw and tongue are prerequisites for a dental *d.*

Skill in articulating this dental *d* will be the best preparation for learning how to flip and roll an Italian *r.*

Practicing Dental Single *d*

A single *d* is short, no matter what its position in the word.

EXERCISE I: Initial *d* and Single *d* between Vowels

Speak, then sing, using a dental fully voiced *d:*

[diiiidiiiidiiii] [duuuuduuuuduuuu]
[deeeedeeeedeeee] [doooodoooodoooo]
[dɛɛɛɛdɛɛɛɛdɛɛɛɛ] [dɔɔɔɔdɔɔɔɔdɔɔɔɔ]
[dɑɑɑɑdɑɑɑɑdɑɑɑɑ]

Drop the jaw and tongue merely by relaxing them and shape the lips according to the vowel.

To say the *d,* raise the tip of the tongue to the upper front teeth and, as soon as contacted, exert a slight resistance. This should induce the vocal cords to vibrate immediately, as required. Energetically flip the tip of the tongue down to start the vowel.

In spite of its complex articulation, a single *d* must be short. First practice this exercise eliminating all *d*'s and speaking long vowels in continuity. Later add the *d*'s but making certain that they practically do not interrupt the strong vowel line.

Since the Italian *d* is fully voiced, a pitch should be audible during the entire exercise.

REMARK ON FINAL *d*

In Italian the consonant *d* does not occur in a final position except for the preposition *ad* ['ɑd] and the conjunctions *ed* ['ed] and *od* ['od] which are sometimes used instead of *a, e* and *o.*

These monosyllables, however, are never final in the phrase, and since they appear only when followed by a vowel, the *d* should be treated like a single *d* between vowels.

Further remarks may be found in Part VII, Section 3(C).

EXERCISE II: Single *d* Words

Speak, then sing, these words using a fully voiced short dental *d.*

(a) INITIAL *d*

An initial *d* should be short and sharp. If one lingers a little on an initial *d,* one is apt to start the word with a *nd,* instead of with a well-enunciated plosive *d.*

deh ['dɛ]
Dio ['diːɔ]
dare ['dɑɾɛ]
degno ['deɲɔ]
dardo ['dɑrdɔ]
destra ['dɛstrɑ]
desio [dɛ'ziːɔ]
dolore [dɔ'loɾɛ]

delirio [dɛ'liɾjɔ]
diletto [di'lɛttɔ]
delizia [dɛ'litsjɑ]
deforme [dɛ'formɛ]
davvero [dɑv'veɾɔ]
demone ['dɛmɔnɛ]
diavolo ['djɑvɔlɔ]
deserto [dɛ'zɛrtɔ]

debolezza [dɛbɔ'lettsɑ]
delitto [dɛ'littɔ]
Despina [dɛ'spinɑ]
Dorabella [dɔɾɑ'bɛllɑ]
Desdemona [dɛ'zdɛmɔnɑ]
Dandini [dɑn'dini]
Dolcina [dɔl'tʃinɑ]
Dulcamara [dulkɑ'mɑɾɑ]

(b) SINGLE *d* BETWEEN VOWELS

odo ['ɔdɔ]
odio ['ɔdjɔ]
lode ['lɔdɛ]

frode ['frɔdɛ]
godo ['gɔdɔ]
modo ['mɔdɔ]

piede ['pjɛdɛ]
bada ['bɑdɑ]
idea [i'dɛːɑ]

idolo ['idɔlɔ]
madido ['mɑdidɔ]
lurido ['luɾidɔ]
godere [gɔ'deɾɛ]
madama [mɑ'dɑmɑ]

assidera [ɑs'sidɛɾɑ]
desiderio [dɛzi'dɛɾjɔ]
adornare [ɑdɔr'nɑɾɛ]
madamina [mɑdɑ'minɑ]
Madonna [mɑ'dɔnnɑ]

Cavaradossi [kɑvɑɾɑ'dɔssi]
Aida [ɑ'idɑ]
Adina [ɑ'dinɑ]
Euridice [ɛ:üɾi'ditʃɛ]
Roderigo [rɔdɛ'ɾigɔ]

(c) *d* NEXT TO A CONSONANT

This *d* too should be dental, voiced, short and in perfect contact with the neighboring consonant. The word is *madre* ['mɑdrɛ], not ['mɑdərɛ], as is sometimes heard.

onde ['ondɛ]
fronda ['frondɑ]
manda ['mɑndɑ]
ardo ['ɑrdɔ]
verde ['verdɛ]
lorde ['lordɛ]
caldo ['kɑldɔ]
madre ['mɑdrɛ]

padre ['pɑdrɛ]
quadro ['kwɑdrɔ]
andare [ɑn'dɑɾɛ]
ardere ['ɑrdɛɾɛ]
soldato [sɔl'dɑtɔ]
perdono [pɛr'donɔ]
tremendo [trɛ'mɛndɔ]
bandolo ['bɑndɔlɔ]

fremebondo [frɛmɛ'bondɔ]
abbandono [ɑbbɑn'donɔ]
riscaldare [riskɑl'dɑɾɛ]
Rodrigo [rɔ'drigɔ]
Adriana [ɑ'drjɑnɑ]
Alcindoro [altʃin'dɔɾɔ]
Fernando [fɛr'nɑndɔ]
Bardolfo [bɑr'dolfɔ]

Practicing Dental Double *d*

To lengthen a double *d,* prolong the second articulatory step, the stop.

Since the double *d* must be as dental and fully voiced as a single one, a pitch should be audible from beginning to end of the double consonant.

EXERCISE

Speak, then sing:

freddo ['freddɔ]
ridda ['riddɑ]
addio [ɑd'di:ɔ]
Iddio [id'di:ɔ]
adduce [ɑd'dutʃɛ]
laddove [lɑd'dovɛ]
addosso [ɑd'dɔssɔ]
suddito ['sudditɔ]
addurre [ɑd'durrɛ]
raddoppio [rɑd'doppjɔ]

addobbare [ɑddɔb'bɑɾɛ]
raddrizzare [rɑddrit'tsɑɾɛ]
soddisfare [sɔddi'sfɑɾɛ]
addomine [ɑd'dɔminɛ]
addormentare [ɑddɔrmɛn'tɑɾɛ]
addolorare [ɑddɔlɔ'ɾɑɾɛ]
Nedda ['nɛddɑ]
Taddeo [tɑd'dɛ:ɔ]
Turiddu [tu'ɾiddu]
Maddalena [mɑddɑ'lɛnɑ]

(D) The Dental *t*

CLASSIFICATION

The Italian *t* is a "dental unaspirated voiceless plosive" consonant (see Chart I).

DISCUSSION

Unlike the English alveolar *t,* the Italian *t* is "dental," and is made with the tip of the tongue touching the inside of the upper front teeth. Thus it is produced farther forward in the mouth than the English *t.*

The Italian *t* is further classified as a "voiceless plosive." The English *t* is also a voiceless plosive but with this difference: English voiceless plosives are "aspirated" (that is, articulated with an escape of breath between the consonant and the following vowel); Italian voiceless plosives are "unaspirated." They are spoken without any puff of air separating them from the following vowel.

Further remarks will be found in Section 4 of Part III dealing with the Voiceless Plosives.

REMARK

As a plosive, the dental *t* requires the same complex action of the tip of the tongue as its voiced counterpart, the *d*—that is, the tip of the tongue first closes the breath passage through firm contact with the upper teeth, holds it closed for an instant, and then suddenly releases the breath by being flipped down quickly to rest against the lower teeth.

In spite of this complex action of the tip of the tongue, there should be no tension in the jaw and the tongue.

Practicing Dental Unaspirated Single *t*

A single *t* is short, no matter what its position in the word.

EXERCISE I: Initial *t* and Single *t* between Vowels

Speak, then sing, using a short dental unaspirated *t*:

[tiiiitiiiitiiii] [tuuuutuuuutuuuu]
[teeeeteeeeteeee] [toooo toooo toooo]
[tɛɛɛɛtɛɛɛɛtɛɛɛɛ] [tuuuutuuuutuuuu]
[tɑɑɑɑtɑɑɑɑtɑɑɑɑ]

Drop the jaw and tongue by relaxing them and shape the lips according to the vowel.

To say a *t,* firmly contact the upper incisors with the tip of the tongue, then energetically separate them. The resulting explosive release of the breath must be immediately vocalized to avoid aspiration.

To learn to say short *t*'s, first eliminate them, seaking only the vowels in continuity. Later add the *t*'s, still maintaining a practically uninterrupted vowel line.

Avoid any distortion of the monophthongs.

REMARK ON FINAL *t*

A final *t* never occurs in Italian.

EXERCISE II: Single *t* Words

Speak, then sing, using a dental unaspirated short single *t*:

(a) INITIAL *t* FOLLOWED BY A VOWEL

tu ['tu]	tino ['tinɔ]	tepore [tɛ'poɾɛ]
tè ['tɛ]	tuono ['twɔnɔ]	tormento [tɔr'mentɔ]
tela ['telɑ]	torneo [tɔr'nɛ:ɔ]	tesoro [tɛ'zɔɾɔ]
tisi ['tizi]	timore [ti'moɾɛ]	turbamento [turbɑ'mentɔ]
testa ['tɛstɑ]	tenero ['tɛnɛɾɔ]	tabernacoli [tɑbɛr'nɑkɔli]
tanto ['tɑntɔ]	tenebre ['tɛnɛbrɛ]	Tom ['tɔm]
tetro ['tɛtrɔ]	tanghero ['tɑŋgɛɾɔ]	Tosca ['tɔskɑ]
tosse ['tossɛ]	taffetà [tɑffɛ'tɑ]	Turandot [tuɾɑn'dɔ]

(b) SINGLE *t* BETWEEN VOWELS

dito ['ditɔ]	fatale [fɑ'tɑlɛ]	catalogo [kɑ'tɑlɔgɔ]
muto ['mutɔ]	fratelli [frɑ'tɛlli]	vincitore [vintʃi'toɾɛ]
moto ['mɔtɔ]	malata [mɑ'lɑtɑ]	scellerato [ʃɛllɛ'ɾɑtɔ]
vuoto ['vwɔtɔ]	segreto [sɛ'gretɔ]	Otello [ɔ'tɛllɔ]
fato ['fɑtɔ]	ritorno [ri'tornɔ]	Melitone [mɛli'tonɛ]
meta ['mɛtɑ]	notaio [nɔ'tɑjɔ]	Favorita [fɑvɔ'ɾitɑ]
seta ['setɑ]	notizia [nɔ'titsjɑ]	Puritani [puɾi'tɑni]
sete ['setɛ]	eterno [ɛ'tɛrnɔ]	Traviata [trɑvi'ɑtɑ]

(c) *t* NEXT TO A CONSONANT

In addition to being short, dental and unaspirated, such a single *t* should be in perfect contact with the adjoining consonant.

conte ['kontɛ]	svelto ['zvɛltɔ]	patente [pɑ'tɛntɛ]
alto ['ɑltɔ]	frusta ['frustɑ]	destino [dɛ'stinɔ]
stolto ['stoltɔ]	gentile [dʒɛn'tilɛ]	frastuono [frɑ'stwɔnɔ]
fasto ['fɑstɔ]	studente [stu'dɛntɛ]	Santuzza [sɑn'tuttsɑ]
casta ['kɑstɑ]	atroce [ɑ'trotʃɛ]	Falstaff ['fɑlstɑff]
tetro ['tɛtrɔ]	straziare [strɑ'tsjɑɾɛ]	Mefistofele [mɛfi'stɔfɛlɛ]
metro ['mɛtrɔ]	illustre [il'lustrɛ]	Bartolo ['bɑrtɔlɔ]
presto ['prɛstɔ]	trionfo [tri'onfɔ]	Cenerentola [tʃɛnɛ'ɾɛntɔlɑ]

PRACTICING DENTAL UNASPIRATED DOUBLE *t*

To lengthen a double *t*, prolong the second articulatory step, the stop. No effort or tension is required or permitted. It is a simple matter of timing and of holding the required position with a relaxed jaw and tongue. When this is achieved, one will be able to say not only a double, but a triple or quadruple *t* without effort. This is an excellent exercise.

Since the *t* is a voiceless plosive, a double *t* interrupts the vibrations of the vocal cords and the vocal line. Although this interferes with smooth vocalization, it should not be avoided since there are words whose meaning changes with the doubling of a *t*. *Note* ['nɔtɛ] means *notes, notte* ['nɔttɛ] means *night*. *Bruto* ['brutɔ] stands for *brute, brutto* ['bruttɔ] for *ugly*.

In spite of the lengthened double *t*, at the release of the breath the vowel must begin immediately and vocalization is restored at once without intermediate aspiration. The double *t* and the vowel that follows are solidly attached to each other.

EXERCISE

Speak, then sing, using a dental unaspirated double *t:*

letto ['lɛttɔ]	saetta [sɑ'ettɑ]	manicotto [mɑni'kɔttɔ]
detto ['dettɔ]	attimo ['ɑttimɔ]	Masetto [mɑ'zettɔ]
botte ['bɔttɛ]	aspetto [ɑ'spɛttɔ]	Musetta [mu'zettɑ]
botte ['bottɛ]	vittima ['vittimɑ]	Violetta [viɔ'lettɑ]
batti ['bɑtti]	sottile [sɔt'tilɛ]	Rigoletto [rigɔ'lettɔ]
brutto ['bruttɔ]	cospetto [kɔ'spɛttɔ]	Angelotti [ɑndʒɛ'lɔtti]
lutto ['luttɔ]	perfetto [pɛr'fɛttɔ]	Attavanti [ɑttɑ'vɑnti]
tetto ['tettɔ]	sospetto [sɔ'spɛttɔ]	Lauretta [lɑːŭ'ɾettɑ]

(E) The Dental *r*

CLASSIFICATION

The Italian *r* is a "dental voiced vibrant" consonant (see Chart I).

DISCUSSION

The Italian *r* has little in common with the American *r*. The American *r* is "alveolar," made with the tip of the tongue not touching, but pointing toward, the back of the upper gum ridge. The Italian *r* is "dental," with the tip of the tongue making actual contact, once or several times, with the top of the inside of the upper incisors where the gum ridge begins.

The American *r* is a "fricative"—that is, a consonant uttered with so narrowed a breath passage that the escaping air produces uniform friction. The Italian *r* is a "vibrant," articulated with the free tip of the tongue vibrating—that is, trilling in and through the breath stream against the top of the upper teeth. For this reason the Italian *r* is said to be tongue tip trilled.

The English *r* is often accompanied by some lip protrusion and upper lip vibration. In articulating the Italian *r* the lips are completely passive.

Whereas the American *r* is not always completely voiced, the Italian *r* is always "fully voiced."

To summarize: unlike the American *r,* the Italian *r* is dental, trilled with the tip of the tongue, uttered without lip vibration and fully voiced.

The Flipped And The Rolled *r*

There are two kinds of *r*'s in Italian, the flipped, also called flapped [ɾ], and the rolled [r].

A flipped *r* is a one-tap *r,* where the tip of the tongue comes in contact only once with the top of the upper teeth. A rolled *r* is made by a quick succession of a number of taps.

How To Learn To Flip And Roll An *r*

Since the Italian *r* is articulated with the tip of the tongue touching the top of the inside of the upper incisors where the gum ridge begins, its point of articulation is slightly higher than with the other dentals.

If one compares the Italian *r* with the other dentals, *l, n, d* and *t,* one will realize that because of the nature of its articulation and sound, the *r* has the greatest affinity with the *d.*

For example, in southern England a flipped *r,* very similar to the Italian, is used as in *very merry*—that is, in words spelled with a single or double *r* between vowels. Sometimes one is unable to determine what is being said: is it *very merry* with a flipped *r* or *veddy meddy* with a dental *d?* The two sounds are so related that it may be difficult to distinguish one from the other.

This shows that a correctly dentalized *d* is the best starting point for learning the Italian flipped *r.* And it also indicates the quickest method for acquiring such an *r,* provided one is a good mimic. Then all one has to do is to imitate the standard British pronunciation of such words as *ferry, torrid, spirit, carol,* etc.

If you are a person who has difficulty in pronouncing an Italian *r,* first practice the flipped *r,* and learn the rolled *r* later.

To flip an *r* jaw and tongue must be relaxed. The tip of the tongue rises and flips—lightly vibrates—against the top of the upper incisors or even a little above. To achieve this flipping, the tip of the tongue must be nimble, flexible and elastic. The muscles of the tip of the tongue must have been developed and trained.

The best way to develop these muscles is through persistent practice of the dental consonants. Do not consider time wasted if, to acquire an *r,* you must repeat the exercises for the dental *l, n, d* and *t,* particularly Exercise I.

As soon as you have complete control of tongue and jaw in speaking Exercise I of the Dental *d,* try to change the [dɑɑɑɑdɑɑɑɑdɑɑɑɑ] to [dɑɑɑɑdɑɑɑɑɾɑɑɑɑ], to [dɑɑɑɑɾɑɑɑɑɾɑɑɑɑ], and finally to [ɾɑɑɑɑɾɑɑɑɑ ɾɑɑɑɑ].

When you feel secure with the flipped *r,* try to extend the flip into flips, which is what a rolled *r* consists of; keep on trying until the muscles of the tip of the tongue respond as they should. It is wise to avoid working for a long period of time, as your muscles will tire and tense. Short, frequent periods of practice are the most beneficial.

Some singers find it easier to learn to roll an *r* by preceding it with a plosive consonant. Try the syllables *traaaa* or *draaaa* or *praaaa* or *braaaa.* Find the syllable in which the tip of the tongue functions best and produces more than one tap. Just two or three are a perfect beginning. Building them into a longer rolled *r* is a matter of patience.

Other singers have first succeeded in rolling an *r* by letting their breath activate the tip of their tongue until it vibrates, for it is the breath that causes the tip of the tongue to trill against the teeth. If necessary try to place the tip of the tongue toward the top of the upper incisors as if to say a *d,* but without actually touching the incisors so as to give the tip of the tongue a chance to vibrate. Then expel your breath suddenly with an energetic jerk. This should not be attempted more than a few times.

When some kind of lingual trill results, practice for short periods until you master the rolled *r*. Remember you will succeed only if the jaw and the tongue are relaxed.

Rules On The Flipping And Rolling Of *r*

An *r* is flipped:

a) when it is single between vowels, as in *dolore* [dɔ'lorɛ], *core* ['kɔrɛ];

b) when final in a word but followed by a vowel within the phrase. Thus, the first *r* in *"Amor, amor, . . ."* [ɑ-'mo-rɑ-'mor] (*La Bohème,* Act I) is flipped (see Part VII on WORDS IN CONTEXT, Section 3(C)).

An *r* is rolled:

a) when initial as in *re* ['re], *ricusai* [riku'zɑːĭ]. (This is not necessarily so in conversation.);

b) when final in many apocopated words such as *onor* [ɔ'nor], *Signor* [si'ɲor], except as in (b) above;

c) when preceding or following another consonant as in *morte* ['mɔrtɛ], *arma* ['ɑrmɑ], *tremo* ['trɛmɔ], *segreto* [sɛ'gretɔ];

d) when double as in *terra* ['tɛrrɑ], *ferro* ['fɛrrɔ].

REMARK

In Italian an *r* followed by a consonant and a final *r* is rolled; thus *dardo* ['dɑrdɔ] and *amor* [ɑ'mor] have a rolled *r*.

English-speaking singers often do not pronounce these *r*'s at all because in standard English an *r* followed by a consonant and a final *r* is silent.

But unlike English, in Italian these *r*'s are not only pronounced, but rolled.

PRACTICING FLIPPED *r*

EXERCISE I: Initial *r* and Single *r* between Vowels

Speak, then sing:

[ɾiiiiɾiiiiɾiiii] [ɾuuuuɾuuuuɾuuuu]
[ɾeeeeɾeeeeɾeeee] [ɾooooɾooooɾoooo]
[ɾɛɛɛɛɾɛɛɛɛɾɛɛɛɛ] [ɾɔɔɔɔɾɔɔɔɔɾɔɔɔɔ]
[ɾɑɑɑɑɾɑɑɑɑɾɑɑɑɑ]

Drop your jaw and tongue by relaxing them. Shape the lips according to the vowel and keep them motionless throughout. Accentuate the smiling position during the pronunciation of the front and low vowels to help eliminate the lip protrusion and vibrations which are characteristic of the English *r*.

Raise the tip of the tongue and flip it against the top of the upper teeth, then let it fall back to start the vowel.

A flipped *r* should be extremely short, as short as a *d*. Concentrate on greatly sustaining the preceding vowel so as not to be tempted to anticipate and lengthen the *r*. Also, use the technique of first eliminating the *r*'s and later restoring them.

EXERCISE II: Flipped *r* Words

ira [ˈiɾɑ]
ora [ˈoɾɑ]
ara [ˈɑɾɑ]
oro [ˈɔɾɔ]
cura [ˈkuɾɑ]
mare [ˈmɑɾɛ]
sera [ˈseɾɑ]
dolore [dɔˈloɾɛ]

furore [fuˈɾoɾɛ]
timore [tiˈmoɾɛ]
morire [mɔˈɾiɾɛ]
parola [pɑˈɾɔlɑ]
piacere [pjɑˈtʃeɾɛ]
stassera [stɑsˈseɾɑ]
fioretti [fjɔˈɾetti]
tesoro [tɛˈzɔɾɔ]

aurora [ɑːŭˈɾɔɾɑ]
Goro [ˈgɔɾɔ]
Moro [ˈmɔɾɔ]
Alvaro [alˈvaɾɔ]
Figaro [ˈfigɑɾɔ]
Cherubino [kɛɾuˈbinɔ]
Sparafucile [spɑɾɑfuˈtʃilɛ]
Semiramide [sɛmiˈɾɑmidɛ]

PRACTICING ROLLED *r*

Practice the rolled *r* only after you have mastered the flipped one.

EXERCISE I

Speak, then sing, using a rolled *r:*

[priiiipriiiipriiii] [pruuuupruuuupruuuu]
[preeeepreeeepreeee] [proooopro ooopro ooo]
[prɛɛɛɛprɛɛɛɛprɛɛɛɛ] [prɔɔɔɔprɔɔɔɔprɔɔɔɔ]
[prɑɑɑɑprɑɑɑɑprɑɑɑɑ]

Do the same with:

[triiiitriiiitriiii], etc. [driiiidriiiidriiii], etc.
[briiiibriiiibriiii], etc.

As with the flipped *r,* the jaw should be relaxed and motionless. The tongue should be loose and nimble. The lips should be in the vowel position before starting each exercise and motionless throughout.

EXERCISE II: Rolled *r* Words

Speak, then sing:

(a) ROLLED INITIAL *r*

re ['re]
rio ['riːɔ]
ramo ['ramɔ]
rogo ['rogɔ]
ridi ['ridi]
ratto ['rattɔ]
raggio ['raddʒɔ]
roveti [rɔ'veti]

rancore [raŋ'koɾɛ]
rumore [ru'moɾɛ]
ricordo [ri'kɔrdɔ]
rimorso [ri'mɔrsɔ]
rinasco [ri'naskɔ]
raffronto [raf'frontɔ]
realtà [rɛal'ta]
ranocchi [ra'nɔkki]

ronzando [rɔn'dzandɔ]
rorido ['rɔɾidɔ]
recitar [rɛtʃi'tar]
reggimento [rɛddʒi'mentɔ]
Riccardo [rik'kardɔ]
Radamès [rada'mɛs]
Rodrigo [rɔ'drigɔ]
Rinuccio [ri'nuttʃɔ]

(b) ROLLED FINAL *r*

Unlike the English, French and German final *r,* the Italian final *r* is rolled, fully voiced and supported to the end.

or ['or]
cor ['kɔr]
mar ['mar]
fior ['fjor]
signor [si'ɲor]
amor [a'mor]
dolor [dɔ'lor]
languor [laŋ'gwor]

furor [fu'ɾor]
timor [ti'mor]
onor [ɔ'nor]
fulgor [ful'gor]
cantor [kan'tor]
orror [ɔr'ror]
cantar [kan'tar]
danzar [dan'tsar]

morir [mɔ'ɾir]
gioir [dʒɔ'ir]
soffrir [sɔf'frir]
veder [vɛ'der]
amar [a'mar]
ancor [aŋ'kor]
recitar [rɛtʃi'tar]
Oscar ['ɔskar]

(c) ROLLED *r* NEXT TO A CONSONANT

Work toward a perfect contact between the rolled *r* and its neighboring consonant. Do not allow a neutral vowel [ə] to separate them.

morte ['mɔrtɛ]
arte ['artɛ]
arma ['arma]
forza ['fɔrtsa]
sfarzo ['sfartsɔ]
sorte ['sɔrtɛ]
acre ['akrɛ]
egro ['ɛgrɔ]

tremo ['trɛmɔ]
crudo ['krudɔ]
parlare [par'laɾɛ]
schernito [skɛr'nitɔ]
ricordo [ri'kɔrdɔ]
martiri [mar'tiɾi]
lagrima ['lagrima]
preghiera [prɛ'gjɛɾa]

carnefice [kar'nefitʃɛ]
Zerlina [dzɛr'lina]
Amonasro [amɔ'nazrɔ]
Andrea [an'drɛːa]
Adriana [a'drjana]
Ernani [ɛr'nani]
Orfeo [ɔr'fɛːɔ]
Ulrica [ul'rika]

(d) ROLLED DOUBLE *r*

A double *r* is longer than an initial, a final rolled *r* or a rolled *r* next to a consonant. It has the length of two rolled *r*'s, one to be sung on the pitch of the preceding vowel, the other on the pitch of the following vowel. There should be no break.

Energetically shorten the preceding vowel so as to have the time to adequately roll the double *r*.

terra ['tɛrrɑ]	errore [ɛr'roɾɛ]	terrore [tɛr'roɾɛ]
serra ['sɛrrɑ]	zimarra [dzi'mɑrrɑ]	terribile [tɛr'ribilɛ]
ferro ['fɛrrɔ]	correre ['korrɛɾɛ]	serrature [sɛrrɑ'tuɾɛ]
sgherro ['zgɛrrɔ]	carrozza [kɑr'rɔttsɑ]	irrisione [irri'zjonɛ]
sbirri ['zbirri]	corrucci [kɔr'ruttʃi]	Sciarrone [ʃɑr'ronɛ]
guerra ['gwɛrrɑ]	orrido ['ɔrridɔ]	Tabarro [tɑ'bɑrrɔ]
sgarra ['zgɑrrɑ]	orrendo [ɔr'rɛndɔ]	Ferrando [fɛr'rɑndɔ]
azzurro [ɑd'dzurrɔ]	orrore [ɔr'roɾɛ]	Curra ['kurrɑ]

Following are words whose meaning changes with the flipping or rolling of the *r*. Speak, then sing them, proceeding from left to right and differentiating carefully.

caro ['kɑɾɔ] *dear*	carro ['kɑrrɔ] *cart* (n.)
ero ['ɛɾɔ] *I was*	erro ['ɛrrɔ] *I err*
era ['ɛɾɑ] *he was*	erra ['ɛrrɑ] *he errs*
core ['kɔɾɛ] *heart*	corre ['kɔrrɛ] *to gather* (poet.)
fero ['fɛɾɔ] *cruel, proud*	ferro ['fɛrrɔ] *iron* (n.)
aringa [ɑ'ɾiŋgɑ] *herring*	arringa [ɑr'riŋgɑ] *harangue*

4 THE VOICELESS PLOSIVES [p], [t], [k]

In Italian as in English, there are six plosive consonants, three of which, the [p], [t] and [k], are voiceless. The others, the [b], [d] and [g], are voiced.

OUTLINE

Unlike the English voiceless plosives, the Italian [p], [t] and [k] are unaspirated.

For the Unaspirated [p], see Section (A).

For the Unaspirated [t], see Section (B). Since the Italian [t] is dental, see also Section 3 (D).

For the Italian [k], which is Unaspirated and Mediopalatal, see Section (C).

DISCUSSION

Plosive consonants are characterized by a complete stoppage of the flow of breath, followed by a sudden explosive release of the breath.

Three phases may be distinguished in their articulation: (1) the "closure," the coming in contact of the speech organs; (2) the "stop," during which the breath stream is stopped; and (3) the "release," the most audible phase, which occurs when the organs separate and the breath is released.

[p], [t] and [k] are "voiceless plosives"—that is, uttered without vibrations of the vocal cords.

English voiceless plosives are termed "aspirated." When they are followed by a vowel or a pause, there is an audible escape of breath, a puff of air, between the release of the consonant and the vowel or pause. *Pit,* for instance, is actually pronounced ['phɪth]. It consists of three letters but of five speech sounds. And so does *cap* ['khæph]. The [h] following the [p], [t] and [k] symbolizes the aspiration.

Since this aspiration never occurs in Italian, the plosives are called "unaspirated." All the breath released with the third phase of the plosive is converted into vowel sound, and the plosive and the following vowel are in perfect contact.

The difference in sound between aspirated and unaspirated voiceless plosives is striking.

In addition to Italian, French, Spanish and Latin use unaspirated voiceless plosives too.

(A) The Unaspirated [p]

CLASSIFICATION

The Italian [p] is an "unaspirated bilabial voiceless plosive" (see Chart I).

DISCUSSION

The term "bilabial" indicates that the stoppage of the flow of breath is effected by the lips.

The Italian [p] must be "unaspirated." To learn to articulate an unaspirated [p] one should first become aware of the aspiration characteristic of the English [p].

If you say *pie, pen, pull,* you will hear an aspiration—that is, an escape of breath between the plosive and the vowel. If you hold a lighted match in front of your lips while uttering one of these words, the aspiration of the [p] will blow it out.

There is no such escape of breath with an Italian [p]. Thus, while the English *paw* consists of three speech sounds, the [p], the aspiration [h] and the vowel [ɔ], the Italian *po'* ['pɔ] consists of two sounds only, the [p] and the [ɔ].

PRACTICING UNASPIRATED SINGLE [p]

EXERCISE I: Initial [p] Followed by a Vowel

Practice the syllables [pi], [pe], [pɛ], [pɑ], [pɔ], [po], [pu] without aspiration. Enunciate the [p] clearly, using your lips energetically but be sure that at the parting of the lips the vowel starts immediately.

EXERCISE II: Initial [p]

Speak, then sing, avoiding any aspiration:

pane ['pɑnɛ]
pino ['pinɔ]
palo ['pɑlɔ]
pelo ['pelɔ]
pira ['piɾɑ]
pura ['puɾɑ]
poco ['pɔkɔ]
porto ['pɔrtɔ]

pompa ['pompɑ]
paese [pɑ'ezɛ]
paura [pɑ'uɾɑ]
palese [pɑ'lezɛ]
paterno [pɑ'tɛrnɔ]
pazzia [pɑt'tsiːɑ]
patente [pɑ'tɛntɛ]
perfido ['pɛrfidɔ]

possente [pɔs'sɛntɛ]
povero ['pɔveɾɔ]
perdonare [pɛrdɔ'nɑɾɛ]
pentimento [pɛnti'mentɔ]
paravento [pɑɾɑ'vɛntɔ]
Paolo ['pɑːɔlɔ]
Pasquale [pɑ'skwɑlɛ]
Puritani [puɾi'tɑni]

EXERCISE III: Single [p] between Vowels

Sustain the preceding vowel and articulate a [p] so short as not to interrupt the vowel continuity.

Though [p] is voiceless, pretending to sing through a single [p] between vowels will contribute to the continuity of the vowel and vocal lines. It seems to prevent the [p] from breaking up the word and phrase.

Speak, then sing:

epa ['ɛpɑ]
ape ['ɑpɛ]
lupo ['lupɔ]
cupo ['kupɔ]
capo ['kɑpɔ]
papa ['pɑpɑ]
dopo ['dopɔ]
ripa ['ripɑ]

stipo ['stipɔ]
crepa ['krɛpɑ]
capelli [kɑ'pelli]
nipote [ni'potɛ]
aperto [ɑ'pɛrtɔ]
coperto [kɔ'pɛrtɔ]
riposo [ri'pɔzɔ]
dipinto [di'pintɔ]

stupido ['stupidɔ]
stupito [stu'pitɔ]
capitano [kɑpi'tɑnɔ]
sepoltura [sɛpɔl'tuɾɑ]
apoteosi [ɑpɔtɛ'ɔzi]
epicureo [ɛpiku'ɾɛːɔ]
Napata ['nɑpɑtɑ]
Isepo [i'zɛpɔ]

EXERCISE IV: [p] next to a Consonant

Such a [p] should be in perfect contact with the neighboring consonant.

Speak, then sing:

apro ['ɑprɔ]
aspro ['ɑsprɔ]

prode ['prɔdɛ]
prece ['prɛtʃɛ]

plauso ['plɑːŭzɔ]
spada ['spɑdɑ]

spettro ['spɛttrɔ]	speranza [spɛ'rantsa]	risplendere [ri'splɛndɛrɛ]
speme ['spɛmɛ]	prologo ['prɔlɔgɔ]	spettinata [spɛtti'nata]
sprezzo ['sprɛttsɔ]	presago [prɛ'zagɔ]	Ceprano [tʃɛ'pranɔ]
turpe ['turpɛ]	placido ['platʃidɔ]	Serpina [sɛr'pina]
prora ['prɔra]	amplesso [am'plɛssɔ]	Despina [dɛ'spina]
aspide ['aspidɛ]	improvviso [imprɔv'vizɔ]	Principe ['printʃipɛ]

Practicing Unaspirated Double [p]

In a double [p], the phase of the plosive which is prolonged is the stop—that is, the second inaudible phase during which the breath stream is stopped. Thus, with double [p], there must occur an interruption of the vowel and vocal lines in speech as well as in singing. This interruption occurs in Italian only with a double voiceless plosive. It is required in order to distinguish between the meaning of such words as: *copia* ['kɔpja] (*copy*) and *coppia* ['kɔppja] (*couple*), *papa* ['papa] (*pope*) and *pappa* ['pappa] (*pap*).

Doubling a consonant is a matter of timing. Shorten the preceding vowel distinctly and start the first phase, the closure of the [p], immediately so as to have time to linger sufficiently on the stop. Lingering on the stop will not cause any strain if the lips are kept soft and relaxed. When it is time for the release, concentrate upon avoiding any aspiration.

EXERCISE

drappo ['drappɔ]	apparì [appa'ri]	strappare [strap'parɛ]
scoppio ['skɔppjɔ]	appieno [ap'pjɛnɔ]	apposta [ap'pɔsta]
nappo ['nappɔ]	galoppo [ga'lɔppɔ]	applauso [ap'plaːŭzɔ]
pappo ['pappɔ]	approdo [ap'prɔdɔ]	supplice ['supplitʃɛ]
troppo ['trɔppɔ]	appena [ap'pena]	opportuno [ɔppɔr'tunɔ]
ceppo ['tʃeppɔ]	supplizio [sup'plitsjɔ]	Filippo [fi'lippɔ]
gruppo ['gruppɔ]	oppure [ɔp'purɛ]	Peppe ['pɛppɛ]
strappo ['strappɔ]	trappola ['trappɔla]	Giuseppe [dʒu'zɛppɛ]

(B) The Unaspirated [t]

CLASSIFICATION

The Italian [t] is an "unaspirated dental voiceless plosive" (see Chart I).

DISCUSSION

The term "dental" denotes that the stoppage of the stream of breath is effected by the tip of the tongue touching the upper teeth.

To become conscious of the aspiration of the English [t], speak the words *ten, tea, too*. You will hear the escape of breath between the [t] and the vowel. Hold a lighted match in front of your lips while saying one of these words, and the aspiration of the [t] will extinguish it.

There is no such escape of breath with an Italian [t].

While *too* consists of three sounds, the [t], the aspiration [h] and the vowel [u], the Italian *tu* ['tu] consists of two sounds only, the [t] and the [u].

Practicing Unaspirated Dental Single [t]

EXERCISE I: Initial [t] Followed by a Vowel

Practice the Italian syllables [ti], [te], [tɛ], [tɑ], [tɔ], [to], [tu], with no aspiration. Be certain that when the tip of the tongue separates from the teeth, the vowel starts immediately.

EXERCISE II:

Speak, then sing:

tana ['tɑnɑ]	tosto ['tɔstɔ]	torrido ['tɔrridɔ]
tono ['tɔnɔ]	tema ['temɑ]	tempesta [tɛm'pɛstɑ]
tocca ['tokkɑ]	tutore [tu'toɾɛ]	tuberose [tubɛ'ɾɔzɛ]
tempio ['tɛmpjɔ]	tacito ['tɑtʃitɔ]	temerario [tɛmɛ'ɾɑɾjɔ]
tardi ['tɑrdi]	talamo ['tɑlɑmɔ]	tarantella [tɑɾɑn'tɛllɑ]
tondo ['tondɔ]	tamburo [tɑm'buɾɔ]	Tonio ['tɔnjɔ]
tomba ['tombɑ]	timido ['timidɔ]	Turiddu [tu'ɾiddu]
torto ['tɔrtɔ]	torbido ['torbidɔ]	Tancredi [tɑŋ'krɛdi]

EXERCISE III: Single [t] between Vowels

Sustain the preceding vowel and articulate a [t] so short as not to interrupt the vowel continuity.

Though [t] is voiceless, pretending to sing through a single [t] will contribute to the continuity of the vowel and vocal lines. It seems to prevent the [t] from breaking up the word and phrase.

Speak, then sing, avoiding any aspiration and using a dental [t]:

note ['nɔtɛ]	mieto ['mjɛtɔ]	traditore [trɑdi'toɾɛ]
loto ['lɔtɔ]	nato ['nɑtɔ]	mentitore [mɛnti'toɾɛ]
gote ['gɔtɛ]	noto ['nɔtɔ]	sempiterno [sɛmpi'tɛrnɔ]
fate ['fɑtɛ]	tradito [trɑ'ditɔ]	illanguidita [illɑŋgwi'ditɑ]
voto ['votɔ]	visita ['vizitɑ]	fatalità [fɑtɑli'tɑ]
cheto ['ketɔ]	vietare [vjɛ'tɑɾɛ]	Trovatore [trɔvɑ'toɾɛ]
dote ['dɔtɛ]	catene [kɑ'teɾɛ]	Clotilde [klɔ'tildɛ]
lite ['litɛ]	fatale [fɑ'tɑlɛ]	Zita ['tsitɑ]

EXERCISE IV: [t] next to a Consonant

Such a [t] should be unaspirated, dental and in perfect contact with the neighboring consonant.

Speak, then sing:

tre ['tre]	canto ['kantɔ]	tregenda [trɛ'dʒɛnda]
merto ['mɛrtɔ]	strazio ['stratsjɔ]	traditore [tradi'torɛ]
serto ['sɛrtɔ]	scaltro ['skaltrɔ]	trionfale [triɔn'falɛ]
corto ['kortɔ]	artista [ar'tista]	turbamento [turba'mentɔ]
estro ['ɛstrɔ]	astuzia [a'stutsja]	estasiata [ɛstazi'ata]
astro ['astrɔ]	estremo [ɛ'strɛmɔ]	Pistola [pi'stɔla]
mesta ['mɛsta]	tranello [tra'nɛllɔ]	Fenton ['fɛntɔn]
lustro ['lustrɔ]	tramonto [tra'montɔ]	Montano [mɔn'tanɔ]

PRACTICING UNASPIRATED DENTAL DOUBLE [t]

Refer to the Directions for the last Exercises in Sections 3 (D) and 4 (A).

EXERCISE

Avoid any aspiration.

petto ['pɛttɔ]	aspetta [a'spɛtta]	caminetto [kami'nettɔ]
patto ['pattɔ]	diletto [di'lɛttɔ]	minuetto [minu'ettɔ]
batto ['battɔ]	biglietto [bi'ʎettɔ]	gattamorta [gatta'mɔrta]
atto ['attɔ]	attore [at'torɛ]	Musetta [mu'zetta]
tutto ['tuttɔ]	pittore [pit'torɛ]	Spoletta [spɔ'letta]
scritto ['skrittɔ]	tuttora [tut'tora]	Giorgetta [dʒɔr'dʒetta]
netto ['nettɔ]	piuttosto [pjut'tɔstɔ]	Fiammetta [fjam'metta]
boschetto [bɔ'skettɔ]	cottura [kɔt'tura]	Doretta [dɔ'retta]

(C) THE UNASPIRATED [k]

CLASSIFICATION

The Italian [k] is an "unaspirated mediopalatal voiceless plosive" (see Chart I).

DISCUSSION

The term "mediopalatal" indicates that, while the front of the tongue remains in contact with the lower teeth, the stoppage of the breath stream is brought about by the middle of the tongue touching the junction of the hard and soft palate.

This is different from the articulation of the English [k], called a "velar" plosive, because it is made with the back of the tongue against the soft palate.

Actually, the point of articulation of the English [k] varies a little, depending on the vowel that follows. When a front vowel follows, as in *key* or *kit,* the point of contact is nearer the hard palate—a little farther forward in the mouth than with a back vowel, as in *coo* or *could*. The Italian [k], however, is invariably spoken farther forward in the mouth than the English, no matter what vowel follows. This is important in lyric diction, since a [k] which is articulated farther forward enhances the projection of the word.

Another difference between the two [k]'s is the lack of aspiration characteristic of the Italian voiceless plosives. If you say *car, key, cold* you will become aware of an escape of breath between the plosive and the vowel. And if you hold a lighted match in front of your lips while uttering one of these words, the aspiration of the [k] will blow it out.

There is no such escape of breath with an Italian [k]. For example, while the English word *con* consists of four speech sounds ['khɔn], the Italian word *con* ['kɔn] is made of three sounds only.

SPELLING

In Italian the sound [k] may be spelled *c, ch* or *q* and [kk] is spelled *cc, cch, cq* or *qq*.

Practicing Unaspirated Mediopalatal Single [k]

EXERCISE I: Initial [k] Followed by a Vowel

Practice the Italian syllables [ki], [ke], [kɛ], [kɑ], [kɔ], [ko], [ku] using a mediopalatal [k] with no escape of breath whatever. The vowel should start at the instant the tongue separates from the hard palate.

EXERCISE II

Speak, then sing:

chi ['ki]	canto ['kɑntɔ]	cassetto [kɑs'settɔ]
cane ['kɑnɛ]	chitarra [ki'tɑrrɑ]	contessa [kɔn'tessɑ]
chiave ['kjɑvɛ]	chimera [ki'mɛɾɑ]	corona [kɔ'ɾonɑ]
caro ['kɑɾɔ]	carezza [kɑ'ɾettsɑ]	Carlo ['kɑrlɔ]
core ['kɔɾɛ]	capelli [kɑ'pelli]	Cherubino [kɛɾu'binɔ]
capo ['kɑpɔ]	cappella [kɑp'pɛllɑ]	Cassio ['kɑssjɔ]
cupo ['kupɔ]	cagione [kɑ'dʒonɛ]	Calatrava [kɑlɑ'trɑvɑ]
cura ['kuɾɑ]	carità [kɑɾi'tɑ]	Curzio ['kurtsjɔ]

EXERCISE III: Single [k] between Vowels

Sustain the preceding vowel and articulate a [k] so short as not to interrupt the vowel continuity.

Though [k] is voiceless, pretending to sing through a single [k] between vowels will contribute to the continuity of the vowel and vocal lines. This seems to prevent the [k] from breaking up the word and phrase.

Speak, then sing, a mediopalatal, unaspirated [k].

eco ['ɛkɔ]
loco ['lɔkɔ]
foco ['fɔkɔ]
oca ['ɔkɑ]
roco ['rɔkɔ]
fioco ['fjɔkɔ]
pochi ['pɔki]
gioca ['dʒɔkɑ]

amico [ɑ'mikɔ]
nemico [nɛ'mikɔ]
lirico ['liɾikɔ]
acuto [ɑ'kutɔ]
fracasso [frɑ'kɑssɔ]
macabro ['mɑkɑbrɔ]
magnifico [mɑ'ɲifikɔ]
vendicherò [vendikɛ'ɾɔ]

implacabile [implɑ'kɑbilɛ]
Ulrica [ul'rikɑ]
Gioconda [dʒɔ'kondɑ]
Cieca ['tʃɛkɑ]
Angelica [ɑn'dʒɛlikɑ]
Lodovico [lɔdɔ'vikɔ]
Duca ['dukɑ]
Manrico [man'rikɔ]

EXERCISE IV: [k] next to a Consonant

Such a [k] should be mediopalatal, unaspirated and in perfect contact with the neighboring consonant.

acre ['ɑkrɛ]
sacro ['sɑkrɔ]
manco ['mɑŋkɔ]
stanco ['stɑŋkɔ]
arco ['ɑrkɔ]
lurco ['lurkɔ]
fosco ['foskɔ]
crudo ['krudɔ]

croce ['krotʃɛ]
crine ['krinɛ]
crudele [kru'dɛlɛ]
tragedia [trɑ'dʒɛdjɑ]
scariche ['skɑɾikɛ]
scommessa [skɔm'messɑ]
schiamazzo [skjɑ'mɑttsɔ]
creatore [krɛɑ'toɾɛ]

simulacro [simu'lɑkrɔ]
attoscare [attɔ'skɑɾɛ]
arcobaleno [ɑrkɔbɑ'lenɔ]
Fiesco ['fjeskɔ]
Turco ['turkɔ]
Clorinda [klɔ'ɾindɑ]
Clotilde [klɔ'tildɛ]
Dulcamara [dulkɑ'mɑɾɑ]

PRACTICING UNASPIRATED MEDIOPALATAL DOUBLE [k]

Since the phase which is prolonged in a double [k] is the stop itself there will also be an interruption of the vowel and vocal lines, as previously noted with the double [p] and double [t].

Use a mediopalatal [k] and avoid aspiration:

ecco ['ɛkkɔ]
acqua ['ɑkkwɑ]
occhio ['ɔkkjɔ]
sacco ['sɑkkɔ]
smacco ['zmɑkkɔ]
tocca ['tokkɑ]
tacco ['tɑkkɔ]
nacque ['nɑkkwɛ]

macchia ['mɑkkjɑ]
sciocco ['ʃɔkkɔ]
fiacco ['fjɑkkɔ]
spacchi ['spɑkki]
peccato [pɛk'katɔ]
soqquadro [sɔk'kwɑdrɔ]
leccare [lɛk'kɑɾɛ]
staccato [stɑk'katɔ]

schioccare [skjɔk'kɑɾɛ]
sciocchezza [ʃɔk'kettsɑ]
poffarbacco [pɔffɑr'bɑkkɔ]
trabocchetto [trɑbɔk'kettɔ]
Schicchi ['skikki]
Riccardo [rik'kɑrdɔ]
Nabucco [nɑ'bukkɔ]
Boccanegra [ˌbokkɑ'negrɑ]

5 THE VOICED PLOSIVES [b], [d], [g]

OUTLINE

Unlike the English voiced plosives, the Italian [b], [d] and [g] are invariably completely voiced.

For the Fully Voiced [b], see Section (A).

For the Fully Voiced [d], see Section (B). Since the Italian [d] is Dental, see also Section 3(C).

For the Italian [g] which is Fully Voiced and Mediopalatal, see Section (C).

DISCUSSION

The voiced plosives [b], [d] and [g] are counterparts of the voiceless [p], [t] and [k], since the voiced plosives are also characterized by the stoppage of the stream of breath at the same points of articulation. The same three phases of the voiceless plosives are identified in the voiced ones: (1) the "closure," (2) the "stop" and (3) the "release." What distinguishes the voiced from the voiceless plosives are the added vibrations of the vocal cords.

In English speech the voicing of the voiced plosives may be either complete or partial. In colloquial speech it may even be totally lacking.

To illustrate this point, the [b], [d] and [g] in *obey, idiom* and *again* are mostly completely voiced because they occur between vowels which are voiced sounds. At the beginning or end of a phrase, however, these same plosives are only partially voiced. Thus, in the phrase *draw your sword,* the first phase of the initial *d* and the final phase of the final *d* are unvoiced.

This sometimes partial, sometimes total, unvoicing of the English voiced plosives may account for the difficulty that some English-speaking singers encounter in adequately voicing the Italian (or, for that matter, also the French, Spanish and Latin) [b], [d] and [g]. They often make them sound more like unaspirated [p], [t] and [k].

It must be emphasized that if Italian is to sound like Italian the voiced plosives must be "totally voiced." It is such total voicing which is partly responsible for the characteristic euphony of the language.

(A) The Fully Voiced [b]

CLASSIFICATION

The Italian [b] is a "fully voiced bilabial plosive."

The stoppage of the stream of breath is effected by the lips; hence the term "bilabial."

DIRECTIONS

To achieve a "totally voiced" Italian [b], the vocal cords must vibrate through all its phases—closure, stop and release.

To start the vocal cords vibrating at the beginning of the closure, exert an ever so slight resistance of lip against lip, while keeping them soft and relaxed. You should feel and hear your lips and your vocal cords vibrate.

Maintain such vibrations until the [b] is completed. A pitch should be audible throughout the articulation of this consonant.

Compared to the only partially voiced English [b], the Italian [b] may be described as more delicate and resonant.

PRACTICING FULLY VOICED SINGLE [b]

EXERCISE I: Initial [b]

Since a [b] is a plosive, it will have to have the characteristics of a plosive.

Some singers are in the habit of fumbling an initial [b], and of lingering upon its closure so that it sounds like [mb] instead of a well-enunciated plosive [b]. This must be avoided. The word is *bene* ['bɛnɛ], and not *mbene,* etc.

Practice the immediate closure of a neat, fully voiced initial [b] using the syllables [bi], [be], [bɛ], [bɑ], [bɔ], [bo], [bu].

EXERCISE II

Speak, then sing:

bocca ['bokkɑ]
bimba ['bimbɑ]
barca ['bɑrkɑ]
bello ['bɛllɔ]
basta ['bɑstɑ]
bada ['bɑdɑ]
bevi ['bevi]
boia ['bɔjɑ]

buio ['bujɔ]
burla ['burlɑ]
bile ['bilɛ]
baratro ['bɑɾɑtrɔ]
bindolo ['bindɔlɔ]
barone [bɑ'ɾonɛ]
baleno [bɑ'lenɔ]
beviamo [bɛ'vjɑmɔ]

barella [bɑ'ɾɛllɑ]
baciare [bɑ'tʃɑɾɛ]
bambola ['bɑmbɔlɑ]
buffonerie [buffɔnɛ'ɾi:ɛ]
benedizione [bɛnɛdi'tsjonɛ]
Basilio [bɑ'ziljɔ]
Barbiere [bɑr'bjɛɾɛ]
Barbarina [bɑrbɑ'ɾinɑ]

EXERCISE III: Single [b] between Vowels

Sustain the preceding vowel and articulate a [b] so short and fully voiced as not to interrupt the vowel and vocal lines.

Speak, then sing:

obi ['ɔbi]
ruban ['rubɑn]
fiaba ['fjɑbɑ]
cibo ['tʃibɔ]
abile ['ɑbilɛ]
abito ['ɑbitɔ]
abisso [ɑ'bissɔ]
sibilo ['sibilɔ]

libera ['libɛɾɑ]
nobile ['nɔbilɛ]
amabile [ɑ'mɑbilɛ]
affabile [ɑf'fɑbilɛ]
orribile [ɔr'ribilɛ]
aborrita [ɑbɔr'ritɑ]
fremebondo [frɛmɛ'bondɔ]
prelibato [prɛli'bɑtɔ]

vegetabile [vɛdʒɛ'tɑbilɛ]
Ebe ['ɛbɛ]
Eboli ['ɛbɔli]
Uberto [u'bɛrtɔ]
Barnaba ['bɑrnɑbɑ]
Dorabella [dɔɾɑ'bɛllɑ]
Elisabetta [ɛlizɑ'bɛttɑ]
Abigaille [ɑbigɑ'illɛ]

EXERCISE IV: [b] next to a Consonant

Such [b] should be fully voiced and in perfect contact with the neighboring consonant.

Speak, then sing:

alba ['ɑlbɑ]	sbuffo ['zbuffɔ]	bambola ['bɑmbɔlɑ]
sbaglio ['zbɑʎɔ]	oblio [ɔ'bliːɔ]	brontolare [brɔntɔ'lɑɾɛ]
erba ['ɛrbɑ]	albero ['ɑlbɛɾɔ]	ubriaco [ubri'ɑkɔ]
furbo ['furbɔ]	albore [ɑl'boɾɛ]	bramosia [brɑmɔ'ziːɑ]
blando ['blɑndɔ]	bruciare [bru'tʃɑɾɛ]	sbalordito [zbɑlɔr'ditɔ]
brutto ['bruttɔ]	brindisi ['brindizi]	Gabriele [gɑ'brjɛlɛ]
bruno ['brunɔ]	burbero ['burbɛɾɔ]	Rubria ['rubrjɑ]
breve ['brɛvɛ]	imbrogli [im'brɔʎi]	Sonnambula [sɔn'nɑmbulɑ]

Practicing Fully Voiced Double [b]

The phase of the double [b] that is lengthened is the stop. The preceding vowel is shortened.

The lengthened fully voiced [b] will cause an interruption of the vowel line, but not of the vocal line.

EXERCISE

ebbro ['ɛbbrɔ]	rabbia ['rɑbbjɑ]	abbraccio [ɑb'brɑttʃɔ]
babbo ['bɑbbɔ]	febbre ['fɛbbrɛ]	babbino [bɑb'binɔ]
gobbo ['gɔbbɔ]	ebbene [ɛb'bɛnɛ]	gabbati [gɑb'bɑti]
labbro ['lɑbbrɔ]	ubbìa [ub'biːɑ]	abbandono [ɑbbɑn'donɔ]
nebbia ['nebbjɑ]	abbietto [ɑb'bjɛttɔ]	obbligato [ɔbbli'gɑtɔ]
gabbia ['gɑbbjɑ]	ebbrezza [ɛb'brettsɑ]	obbedire [ɔbbɛ'diɾɛ]

(B) The Fully Voiced [d]

CLASSIFICATION

The Italian [d] is a "fully voiced dental plosive."

The stoppage of the stream of breath is accomplished by the tip of the tongue touching the upper teeth; hence the term "dental" (see Chart I).

DIRECTIONS

To obtain a "fully voiced" Italian [d], the vocal cords must vibrate from the beginning of the closure to the end of the release.

Exert a very slight resistance as soon as you touch the inside of your upper teeth with the relaxed tip of the tongue. This should facilitate the onset of the vibrations of the vocal cords. Maintain these vibrations until the [d] is completed, so that voice and pitch are audible throughout the duration of the consonant.

Compared to an only partially voiced English [d], the Italian one will have a more delicate and resonant quality.

Practicing Fully Voiced Single [d]

EXERCISE I: Initial [d]

A [d] is a plosive consonant and should have the characteristics of its kind.

Some singers are in the habit of fumbling an initial [d], and of lingering upon its closure, so that it sounds like [nd] instead of a well-enunciated plosive [d]. This must be avoided. The word is *dolce* [ˈdoltʃɛ] and not *ndolce,* etc.

Practice the immediate closure of a neat dental, fully voiced, initial [d] with the syllables [di], [de], [dɛ], [dɑ], [dɔ], [do], [du].

EXERCISE II

Speak, then sing:

dama [ˈdɑmɑ]	doge [ˈdɔdʒɛ]	destino [dɛˈstinɔ]
danno [ˈdɑnnɔ]	diva [ˈdivɑ]	dozzinale [dɔddziˈnɑlɛ]
dito [ˈditɔ]	duello [duˈɛllɔ]	damigella [dɑmiˈdʒɛllɑ]
dolce [ˈdoltʃɛ]	debole [ˈdebɔlɛ]	desiderio [dɛziˈdɛɾjɔ]
doglie [ˈdɔʎɛ]	dovizia [dɔˈvitsjɑ]	Duca [ˈdukɑ]
dono [ˈdonɔ]	docile [ˈdɔtʃilɛ]	Dottore [dɔtˈtoɾɛ]
desto [ˈdɛstɔ]	disgusto [diˈzgustɔ]	Doretta [dɔˈɾettɑ]
detto [ˈdettɔ]	deforme [dɛˈformɛ]	Duncano [duŋˈkɑnɔ]

EXERCISE III: Single [d] between Vowels

Refer to Section (A), Exercise III.

modo [ˈmɔdɔ]	gode [ˈgɔdɛ]	laudata [lɑːŭˈdɑtɑ]
nodo [ˈnɔdɔ]	cadi [ˈkɑdi]	modestia [mɔˈdɛstjɑ]
grido [ˈgridɔ]	laida [ˈlɑːĭdɑ]	fatidico [fɑˈtidikɔ]
nido [ˈnidɔ]	udire [uˈdiɾɛ]	medesimo [mɛˈdezimɔ]
bada [ˈbɑdɑ]	idolo [ˈidɔlɔ]	Alfredo [ɑlˈfredɔ]
vedo [ˈvedɔ]	adesso [ɑˈdɛssɔ]	Adorno [ɑˈdornɔ]
strida [ˈstridɑ]	adonto [ɑˈdontɔ]	Adalgisa [ɑdɑlˈdʒizɑ]
fede [ˈfedɛ]	medico [ˈmɛdikɔ̀]	Alidoro [ɑliˈdɔɾɔ]

EXERCISE IV: [d] next to a Consonant

Refer to Section (A), Exercise IV.

onda [ˈondɑ]	dardo [ˈdɑrdɔ]	sdegno [ˈzdeɲɔ]
landa [ˈlɑndɑ]	orda [ˈɔrdɑ]	idra [ˈidrɑ]
falda [ˈfɑldɑ]	dramma [ˈdrɑmmɑ]	drago [ˈdrɑgɔ]

mondo ['mondɔ]	disdire [di'zdirɛ]	Andrea [ɑn'drɛːɑ]
ladro ['lɑdrɔ]	disdegno [di'zdeɲɔ]	Clotilde [klɔ'tildɛ]
ardore [ɑr'dorɛ]	offendere [ɔf'fɛndɛrɛ]	Edgardo [ɛd'gɑrdɔ]
domanda [dɔ'mɑndɑ]	sorprendere [sɔr'prɛndɛrɛ]	Raimondo [rɑːĭ'mondɔ]
mandorlo ['mɑndɔrlɔ]	Fedra ['fɛdrɑ]	Gherardo [gɛ'rɑrdɔ]

Practicing Fully Voiced Double [d]

The phase of the double [d] that is lengthened is the stop.

Since the double [d] is voiced throughout, it will cause an interruption of the vowel line but not of the vocal line.

EXERCISE

Speak, then sing:

addì [ɑd'di]	addentare [ɑddɛn'tɑrɛ]
ridda ['riddɑ]	addobbare [ɑddɔb'bɑrɛ]
freddo ['freddɔ]	addiverrà [ɑddivɛr'rɑ]
addetto [ɑd'dettɔ]	addomine [ɑd'dɔminɛ]
suddetto [sud'dettɔ]	Taddeo [tɑd'dɛːɔ]
raddolcire [rɑddɔl'tʃirɛ]	Maddalena [mɑddɑ'lɛnɑ]

(C) The Fully Voiced [g]

CLASSIFICATION

The Italian [g] is a "fully voiced mediopalatal plosive."

The closure of the breath passage occurs when the middle of the tongue touches the middle of the palate, hence the term "mediopalatal" (see Chart I).

DIRECTIONS

In contrast to the English "velar" [g], the Italian "mediopalatal" [g] is made with the middle of the tongue touching the junction of the hard and soft palates.

To obtain a fully voiced Italian [g], the vocal cords must vibrate through all of its three phases. With a relaxed tongue, exert an ever so slight resistance when first touching the palate. You should feel and hear your vocal cords vibrate; maintain this throughout the duration of the consonant.

Because of its full voicing, and because its point of articulation is farther forward, the Italian [g] has a more delicate and resonant character than the English.

SPELLING

In Italian the [g] sound may be spelled *g* or *gh*.

Practicing Fully Voiced Single [g]

EXERCISE I: Initial [g]

Touch the junction of the hard and soft palates with the middle of the tongue and voice the [g] throughout.

gara ['gɑɾɑ]
gaia ['gɑjɑ]
gazza ['gɑddzɑ]
gola ['golɑ]
gote ['gɔtɛ]
gobbo ['gɔbbɔ]
goccia ['gottʃɑ]
gusto ['gustɔ]

guscio ['guʃɔ]
gavotta [gɑ'vɔttɑ]
galoppo [gɑ'lɔppɔ]
gazzetta [gɑd'dzettɑ]
godẹre [gɔ'deɾɛ]
goloso [gɔ'lozɔ]
gondola ['gondɔlɑ]
gonfiare [gɔn'fjɑɾɛ]

gorgheggio [gɔr'geddʒɔ]
gustare [gu'stɑɾɛ]
ghinea [gi'nɛːɑ]
ghermire [gɛr'miɾɛ]
ghirlanda [gir'lɑndɑ]
Goro ['gɔɾɔ]
Gherardino [gɛɾɑr'dinɔ]
Gabriello [gɑ'brjɛllɔ]

EXERCISE II: Single [g] between Vowels

Sustain the preceding vowel and articulate a [g] so short and fully voiced as not to interrupt the vowel and vocal lines.

Speak, then sing:

foga ['fogɑ]
vaga ['vɑgɑ]
rogo ['rogɔ]
lago ['lɑgɔ]
streghe ['stregɛ]
biga ['bigɑ]
daga ['dɑgɑ]
sfogo ['sfogɔ]

luogo ['lwɔgɔ]
regata [rɛ'gɑtɑ]
fegato ['fegɑtɔ]
agone [ɑ'gonɛ]
affogo [ɑf'fogɔ]
laguna [lɑ'gunɑ]
legare [lɛ'gɑɾɛ]
pagare [pɑ'gɑɾɛ]

elegante [ɛlɛ'gɑntɛ]
aguzzare [ɑgut'tsɑɾɛ]
invaghita [invɑ'gitɑ]
agognare [ɑgɔ'ɲɑɾɛ]
Jago ['jɑgɔ]
Frugola ['frugɔlɑ]
Roderigo [rɔdɛ'ɾigɔ]
Abigaille [ɑbigɑ'illɛ]

EXERCISE III: [g] next to a Consonant

Refer to Section (A), Exercise IV.

grazia ['grɑtsjɑ]
grido ['gridɔ]
magra ['mɑgrɑ]
egro ['ɛgrɔ]
tergo ['tɛrgɔ]
gloria ['glɔrjɑ]

sgherri ['zgɛrri]
sgarra ['zgɑrrɑ]
allegro [ɑl'legrɔ]
letargo [lɛ'tɑrgɔ]
albergo [ɑl'bɛrgɔ]
borghese [bɔr'gezɛ]

gracile ['grɑtʃilɛ]
grembiale [grɛm'bjɑlɛ]
grattacapi [grɑttɑ'kɑpi]
sagrestano [sɑgrɛ'stɑnɔ]
Vargas ['vɑrgɑs]
Margherita [mɑrgɛ'ɾitɑ]

Practicing Fully Voiced Double [g]

The phase of the double [g] that is lengthened is the stop. Since the double [g] is fully voiced, it will cause an interruption of the vowel line, but not of the vocal line.

EXERCISE

leggo ['lɛggɔ]	suggo ['suggɔ]	agguato [ɑg'gwɑtɔ]
reggo ['rɛggɔ]	struggo ['struggɔ]	agguanto [ɑg'gwɑntɔ]
veggo ['veggɔ]	sogghigno [sɔg'giɲɔ]	aggressore [ɑggrɛs'sorɛ]
fuggo ['fuggɔ]	agghiaccia [ɑg'gjɑttʃɑ]	aggredire [ɑggrɛ'dirɛ]
seggo ['sɛggɔ]	aggrada [ɑg'grɑdɑ]	aggrappare [ɑggrɑp'pɑrɛ]
segga ['sɛggɑ]	soggolo [sɔg'golɔ]	aggrovigliare [ɑggrɔvi'ʎɑrɛ]

6 VOICING AND UNVOICING OF *s* AND *z*

OUTLINE

s and *z* are unphonetic letters since each corresponds to two sounds, one voiceless and the other voiced.

The voiceless Italian *s* sounds like the *s* in the English *sun, sand.* It is phonetically symbolized as [s].

The voiced Italian *s* sounds like the *s* in the English *rose, music.* It is phonetically symbolized as [z].

The voiceless Italian letter *z* sounds like the two final consonants in the English *pats, fats,* phonetically symbolized as [ts].

The voiced Italian letter *z* sounds like the two final consonants in the English *pads, fads,* phonetically symbolized as [dz].

Notice that, in Italian, voiced or voiceless, the letter *s* stands for a single sound, either [s] or [z]; but the letter *z,* whether voiced or voiceless, stands for a compound sound, [ts] or [dz].

(A) THE VOICELESS *s*

CLASSIFICATION

The [s] (as in the English *soul*) is a "voiceless dental fricative" (see Chart I).

A "fricative" is a consonant produced by the audible friction of air against some surface of the organs of articulation (in the case of [s], against the ridge of the upper front teeth).

DIRECTIONS

The only difference between the English and the Italian [s] lies in the greater intensity of the Italian [s] which results in a more penetrating hiss.

WHEN TO UNVOICE AN *s*

The five positions in which the letter *s* must be unvoiced are:

1) when initial and followed by a vowel or semiconsonant, as in *sole* ['solɛ], *siete* ['sjɛtɛ],

2) when preceding a voiceless consonant, as in *spada* ['spɑdɑ],
3) when following a consonant, whether voiced or unvoiced, as in *ansia* ['ɑnsjɑ],
4) when doubled, as in *tosse* ['tossɛ],
5) and when final, as in *Radamès* [rɑdɑ'mɛs].

Practicing Voiceless *s*

Speak, then sing:

(1) *s* VOICELESS WHEN INITIAL FOLLOWED BY VOWEL OR SEMICONSONANT

sa ['sɑ]	soave [sɔ'ɑvɛ]	supplizio [sup'plitsjɔ]
su ['su]	sorella [sɔ'ɾɛllɑ]	sigillo [si'dʒillɔ]
seno ['senɔ]	salice ['sɑlitʃɛ]	sacerdoti [sɑtʃɛr'dɔti]
salce ['sɑltʃɛ]	segreto [sɛ'gretɔ]	salvacondotto [ˌsɑlvɑkɔn'dottɔ]
sempre ['sɛmprɛ]	sereno [sɛ'ɾenɔ]	Santa ['sɑntɑ]
suono ['swɔnɔ]	supremo [su'prɛmɔ]	Silva ['silvɑ]
suolo ['swɔlɔ]	sonoro [sɔ'nɔɾɔ]	Siviglia [si'viʎɑ]
siamo ['sjɑmɔ]	suicidio [suːĭ'tʃidjɔ]	Susanna [su'zɑnnɑ]

REMARK

While in Italian an initial *s* followed by a vowel is voiceless, in German it is voiced, as in *Seele* ['zeːlə], *Sohn* ['zoːn]. This may give rise to confusion. In Italian the initial *s* preceding a vowel is voiceless.

(2) *s* VOICELESS WHEN PRECEDING A VOICELESS CONSONANT

speme ['spɛmɛ]	desto ['dɛstɔ]	splendere ['splɛndɛɾɛ]
sposa ['spɔzɑ]	nastro ['nɑstrɔ]	straniero [strɑ'njɛɾɔ]
sforzo ['sfɔrtsɔ]	aspide ['ɑspidɛ]	straziare [strɑ'tsjɑɾɛ]
stanza ['stantsɑ]	maschera ['mɑskɛɾɑ]	struggere ['struddʒɛɾɛ]
scherzo ['skertsɔ]	respiro [rɛ'spiɾɔ]	sagrestano [sɑgrɛ'stɑnɔ]
schiava ['skjɑvɑ]	risposta [ri'spostɑ]	Spoletta [spɔ'lettɑ]
pesca ['peskɑ]	proposta [prɔ'postɑ]	Francesca [fran'tʃeskɑ]
fasto ['fɑstɔ]	squallido ['skwɑllidɔ]	Sparafucile [ˌspɑɾɑfu'tʃilɛ]

(3) *s* VOICELESS WHEN FOLLOWING A CONSONANT

falso ['fɑlsɔ]	arse ['ɑrsɛ]	ansante [ɑn'sɑntɛ]
salsa ['sɑlsɑ]	farsa ['fɑrsɑ]	insidia [in'sidjɑ]
morso ['mɔrsɔ]	senso ['sɛnsɔ]	ansioso [ɑn'sjozɔ]
corso ['korsɔ]	psiche ['psikɛ]	soccorso [sɔk'korsɔ]
forse ['forsɛ]	pensiero [pɛn'sjɛɾɔ]	consiglio [kɔn'siʎɔ]

consenso [kɔn'sɛnsɔ]	insensato [insɛn'sɑtɔ]	Borsa ['borsɑ]
balsamo ['bɑlsɑmɔ]	ansimare [ɑnsi'mɑɾɛ]	Alfonso [ɑl'fonsɔ]
insolente [insɔ'lɛntɛ]	Bersi ['bɛrsi]	Perside ['pɛrsidɛ]

(4) *s* VOICELESS WHEN DOUBLED

In addition to being voiceless, a double *s* is a double consonant in its own right. But quite often a singer who has acquired the skill of prolonging other double consonants fails to do so with a double *s*.

In the following words, make a point of shortening the preceding vowel and lengthening the double *s*.

basso ['bɑssɔ]	chiasso ['kjɑssɔ]	accesso [ɑt'tʃɛssɔ]
lasso ['lɑssɔ]	stesso ['stessɔ]	addosso [ɑd'dɔssɔ]
passo ['pɑssɔ]	essere ['ɛssɛɾɛ]	assassino [ɑssɑs'sinɔ]
spesso ['spessɔ]	assedio [ɑs'sɛdjɔ]	pettirosso [pɛtti'ɾossɔ]
messa ['messɑ]	rossore [rɔs'soɾɛ]	assidera [ɑs'sidɛɾɑ]
rosso ['rossɔ]	possente [pɔs'sɛntɛ]	assentire [ɑssɛn'tiɾɛ]
ossa ['ɔssɑ]	missione [mis'sjonɛ]	Cassio ['kɑssjɔ]
fisso ['fissɔ]	commosso [kɔm'mɔssɔ]	Badessa [bɑ'dessɑ]

(5) *s* VOICELESS WHEN FINAL

There are no Italian words ending with *s*. But there are some well-known operatic characters whose names (not Italian) end with an *s*. The final *s* must be unvoiced.

Radamès [rɑdɑ'mɛs]	Iris ['iɾis]
Ramfis ['rɑmfis]	Cajus ['kɑjus]
Amneris [ɑm'nɛɾis]	Vargas ['vɑrgɑs]
Ines ['inɛs]	

(B) The Voiced *s*

CLASSIFICATION

The [z], as in the English *praise,* is a "voiced dental fricative" (see Chart I).

It is the voiced counterpart of [s] and is produced in the same way, except that with [z] the vocal cords are made to vibrate.

WHEN TO VOICE AN *s*

The Italian letter *s* is voiced in two positions:

1) when preceding a voiced consonant, as in *sdegno* ['zdeɲɔ],

2) when single between vowels, as in *rosa* ['rɔzɑ] (also, see Appendix II).

Practicing Voiced *s*

Speak, then sing:

(1) *s* VOICED WHEN PRECEDING A VOICED CONSONANT

smania ['zmɑnjɑ]	sgonnella [zgɔn'nɛllɑ]	disgusto [di'zgustɔ]
sguardo ['zgwɑrdɔ]	sgomento [zgɔ'mentɔ]	disgraziata [dizgrɑ'tsjɑtɑ]
sdegno ['zdeɲɔ]	sventata [zvɛn'tɑtɑ]	bisbigliare [bizbi'ʎɑɾɛ]
snello ['znɛllɔ]	sgorgare [zgɔr'gɑɾɛ]	cicisbeo [tʃitʃi'zbɛːɔ]
svelto ['zvɛltɔ]	sventura [zvɛn'tuɾɑ]	Tisbe ['tizbɛ]
sgherri ['zgɛrri]	svenevole [zvɛ'nevɔlɛ]	Israele [izrɑ'ɛlɛ]
sgelo ['zdʒɛlɔ]	fantasma [fɑn'tɑzmɑ]	Amonasro [ɑmɔ'nɑzrɔ]
cosmo ['kɔzmɔ]	disdegno [di'zdeɲɔ]	Desdemona [dɛ'zdɛmɔnɑ]

(2) *s* VOICED WHEN SINGLE BETWEEN VOWELS

sposa ['spɔzɑ]	paese [pɑ'ezɛ]	disinvolto [dizin'vɔltɔ]
uso ['uzɔ]	palese [pɑ'lezɛ]	esecrabile [ɛzɛ'krɑbilɛ]
oso ['ɔzɔ]	marchese [mɑr'kezɛ]	Buoso ['bwɔzɔ]
muso ['muzɔ]	deserto [dɛ'zɛrtɔ]	Rosina [rɔ'zinɑ]
viso ['vizɔ]	poesia [pɔɛ'ziːɑ]	Basilio [bɑ'ziljɔ]
vaso ['vɑzɔ]	desio [dɛ'ziːɔ]	Teseo [tɛ'zɛːɔ]
causa ['kɑːŭzɑ]	esule ['ɛzulɛ]	Alvise [ɑl'vizɛ]
asilo [ɑ'zilɔ]	esultate [ɛzul'tɑtɛ]	Teresa [tɛ'ɾɛzɑ]

REMARK ON THE LENGTH OF INTERVOCALIC [z]

The intervocalic [z] is always short—that is, it is always spelled with a single *s*, never with a double one.

Some English-speaking singers tend to prolong it unduly.

Like any single consonant between vowels, the [z] must be neat and short to the point of not interrupting the vowel line.

REMARK ON INTERVOCALIC *s* WITHIN A COMPOUND WORD

Italian has a number of compound words containing an *s* which appears to the eye to be medial between vowels. But it is actually the initial *s* of the second part of the word.

The word *risorto* [ri'sortɔ] consists of the prefix *ri* (*again*) and the verb *sorto* ['sortɔ] (*risen*). Consequently, the *s*, which appears to be single between vowels, is really an initial *s* followed by a vowel and is unvoiced.

Following are other compound words belonging to the same category.

dicesi ['ditʃɛsi] (poetic for *si dice*)	volgasi ['vɔlgɑsi] (poetic for *si volga*)
partasi ['pɑrtɑsi] (poetic for *si parta*)	trasalire [trɑsɑ'liɾɛ]
	trasognato [trɑsɔ'ɲɑtɔ]

risanare [risɑ'nɑɾɛ]
risuonò [riswɔ'nɔ]
risentito [risɛn'titɔ]
risurrezione [risurrɛ'tsjonɛ]
risuscitato [risuʃi'tɑtɔ]

(C) THE VOICELESS *z*

CLASSIFICATION

The voiceless *z*, pronounced [ts] (as in *bits*), is a "voiceless dental affricate" (see Chart I).

An "affricate" consists of a plosive consonant (in this instance the [t]), followed by a fricative (the [s]). The articulation of the plosive is incomplete, for the third phase, the release, does not take place. Instead, because of a slower and looser parting of the speech organs, the fricative is formed.

DIRECTIONS

Because the Italian *t* is dental, the entire articulation of [ts] takes place at the upper front teeth. This is farther forward in the mouth than the English gum ridge [ts].

WHEN TO UNVOICE THE LETTER *z*

Since it is impossible to determine from the spelling when the letter *z* should be voiced or unvoiced in Italian, a dictionary must be consulted.

PRACTICING VOICELESS *z*

Speak, then sing:

EXERCISE I: Voiceless Initial *z*

zio ['tsiːɔ]
zia ['tsiːɑ]
zitto ['tsittɔ]
zoppo ['tsɔppɔ]
zeppo ['tseppɔ]
zuffa ['tsuffɑ]
zampa ['tsɑmpɑ]
zecca ['tsekkɑ]
zana ['tsɑnɑ]
zanna ['tsɑnnɑ]
zecchino [tsɛk'kinɔ]
zimbello [tsim'bɛllɔ]
zucchero ['tsukkɛɾɔ]
zampillo [tsɑm'pillɔ]
zampogna [tsɑm'poɲɑ]
zitella [tsi'tɛllɑ]
zittire [tsit'tiɾɛ]
Zita ['tsitɑ]

EXERCISE II: Voiceless Medial *z*

ozio ['ɔtsjɔ]
grazia ['grɑtsjɑ]
vizio ['vitsjɔ]
scalzo ['skɑltsɔ]
balzo ['bɑltsɔ]
stanza ['stɑntsɑ]
danza ['dɑntsɑ]
sfarzo ['sfɑrtsɔ]
azione [ɑ'tsjonɛ]
nuziale [nu'tsjɑlɛ]
canzone [kɑn'tsonɛ]
tenzone [tɛn'tsonɛ]
dovizie [dɔ'vitsjɛ]
delizia [dɛ'litsjɑ]
novizia [nɔ'vitsjɑ]
Fazio ['fɑtsjɔ]
Fabrizio [fɑ'britsjɔ]
Firenze [fi'ɾɛntsɛ]

EXERCISE III: Voiceless Double *z*

To double a voiceless *z* the plosive [t] is lengthened.

Some singers have difficulty in saying the [s] after [tt]. As a result the double *z* sounds more like a double plosive than the double affricate it is.

Speak, then sing, concentrating on a [tt] followed by an audibly sustained continuant [s]. It will be helpful at the beginning to exaggerate the length of the [s]. To have sufficient time for both lengthened consonants the preceding vowel should be greatly shortened.

nozze ['nɔttsɛ]	stizza ['stittsɑ]	carezza [kɑ'ɾettsɑ]
vezzo ['vettsɔ]	prezzo ['prɛttsɔ]	dolcezza [dɔl'tʃettsɑ]
vezzi ['vettsi]	pizzica ['pittsikɑ]	palazzo [pɑ'lɑttsɔ]
sozzo ['sottsɔ]	stuzzica ['stuttsikɑ]	singhiozzo [siŋ'gjottsɔ]
pozzo ['pottsɔ]	ruzzola ['ruttsɔlɑ]	aguzza [ɑ'guttsɑ]
pazzo ['pɑttsɔ]	bellezza [bɛl'lettsɑ]	fazzoletto [fɑttsɔ'lettɔ]

(D) The Voiced *z*

CLASSIFICATION

The voiced *z*, pronounced [dz] (as in *bids*), is a "voiced dental affricate" (see Chart I). As an affricate, it consists of the voiced plosive [d] followed by the fricative [z]. The third phase of the [d], the release, does not take place. Instead, the related fricative [z] is formed.

DIRECTIONS

Because the Italian *d* is dental, the entire articulation of [dz] takes place at the upper front teeth. This is farther forward in the mouth than the English gum ridge [dz].

WHEN TO VOICE THE LETTER *z*

There is no way to determine when the letter *z* should be voiced in Italian, except by consulting a dictionary.

Practicing Voiced *z*

Speak, then sing:

EXERCISE I: Voiced Initial *z*

zelo ['dzɛlɔ]	zaffiro ['dzɑffiɾɔ]	zerbino [dzɛr'binɔ]
zero ['dzɛɾɔ]	zeffiro ['dzɛffiɾɔ]	zendale [dzɛn'dɑlɛ]
zolla ['dzɔllɑ]	zimarra [dzi'mɑrrɑ]	Zerlina [dzɛr'linɑ]
zeta ['dzɛtɑ]	zelante [dzɛ'lɑntɛ]	Zelatrice [dzɛlɑ'tritʃɛ]
zonzo ['dzondzɔ]	zotico ['dzɔtikɔ]	

EXERCISE II: Voiced Medial *z*

Few words have a voiced medial single *z*.

bonzo ['bondzɔ]	garzone [gɑr'dzonɛ]	azalea [ɑdzɑ'lɛːɑ]
garza ['gɑrdzɑ]	romanzo [rɔ'mɑndzɔ]	Suzuki [su'dzuki]
pranzo ['prɑndzɔ]	donzella [dɔn'dzɛllɑ]	Azucena [ɑdzu'tʃɛnɑ]

EXERCISE III: Voiced Double *z*

To double a voiced *z*, the plosive [d] is lengthened.

To have sufficient time for a double *d* and the continuant [z], adequately shorten the preceding vowel.

mezzo ['mɛddzɔ]	mezzodì [mɛddzɔ'di]	gazzetta [gɑd'dzettɑ]
rozzo ['roddzɔ]	olezzo [ɔ'leddzɔ]	olezzare [ɔled'dzɑrɛ]
grezzo ['greddzɔ]	azzurro [ɑd'dzurrɔ]	orizzonte [ɔrid'dzontɛ]
bizza ['biddzɑ]	bizzarro [bid'dzɑrrɔ]	mezzanotte [ˌmɛddzɑ'nɔttɛ]
gazza ['gɑddzɑ]	dozzina [dɔd'dzinɑ]	mezzosoprano [ˌmɛddzɔsɔ'prɑnɔ]

7 DUAL PRONUNCIATION OF *c*, *g* AND *sc*

OUTLINE

The consonants *c*, *g* and the consonant group *sc* are unphonetic and have two different pronunciations, depending on the letter that follows.

When followed by *a*, *o*, *u*, *l* or *r*, the letter *c* has the simple sound [k] as in *key*. But when followed by *e* or *i*, it stands for the compound sound [tʃ] as in *chair*.

When followed by *a*, *o*, *u*, *l* or *r*, the letter *g* has the simple sound [g] as in *good*. When followed by *e* or *i*, however, it stands for the compound sound [dʒ] as in *jeer*.

When followed by *a*, *o*, *u*, *l* or *r*, the group *sc* stands for the compound sound [sk] as in *skin*. But when followed by *e* or *i*, it has the simple sound [ʃ] as in *shoe*.

DISCUSSION

When preceding the letter *a*, *o*, *u*, *l* or *r*, the consonants *c*, *g* and *sc* have the "hard," "mediopalatal" sound of [k] as in *key*, [g] as in *good* and [sk] as in *skin*. Because they harden a preceding *c*, *g* or *sc*, the vowels *a*, *o* and *u* are called "hardening vowels."

Conversely, whenever preceding *e* or *i*, the consonants *c*, *g* and *sc* have the "soft," "prepalatal" sound of [tʃ] as in *chair*, [dʒ] as in *jeer* and [ʃ] as in *shoe*. The term prepalatal indicates that these consonants are produced at the front part of the hard palate. Since they soften a preceding *c*, *g* or *sc*, the vowels *e* and *i* are called "softening vowels."

Whenever *c, g* or *sc* has the hard, mediopalatal pronunciation, even though it precedes one of the softening vowels *e* or *i,* the letter *h* is inserted, as in *che* ['kɛ], *laghi* ['lɑgi], *scherzo* ['skertsɔ]. The letter *h* is always silent in Italian. Here it is used as a distinguishing sign—that is, a "diacritical mark," without a sound value of its own.

When, however, *c, g* or *sc* has the soft, prepalatal pronunciation, even though preceding one of the hardening vowels *a, o* or *u,* the letter *i* is inserted as a diacritical mark, as in *ciò* ['tʃɔ], *già* ['dʒɑ] and *scialo* ['ʃɑlɔ]. In this particular position the *i* is silent. This is the only instance when a vowel is silent in Italian.

CHART FOR THE PRONUNCIATION OF *c, g* AND *sc*

Hardening Vowels					Softening Vowels	
a	o	u			e	i
ca	co	cu	(car)	[k]	c~~h~~e	c~~h~~i
c~~i~~a	c~~i~~o	c~~i~~u	(child)	[tʃ]	ce	ci
ga	go	gu	(go)	[g]	g~~h~~e	g~~h~~i
g~~i~~a	g~~i~~o	g~~i~~u	(jar)	[dʒ]	ge	gi
sca	sco	scu	(sky)	[sk]	sc~~h~~e	sc~~h~~i
sc~~i~~a	sc~~i~~o	sc~~i~~u	(shoe)	[ʃ]	sce	sci

In the chart above the syllables have been aligned horizontally according to sound, not spelling.

The letter *i* following *c, g* or *sc* and preceding a hardening vowel has been crossed out to symbolize that it is silent. The letter *h,* though invariably silent in Italian, has also been crossed out.

THE SILENT *i*

To avoid confusion as to when or when not the letter *i* should be pronounced, the following chart points out where only a silent *i* may occur.

c		a
g	~~i~~	o
sc		u

It is the *i* or *h* immediately following the *c, g* or *sc* that influences its pronunciation, even though it is silent. But whatever letter follows the *i* or *h* is there in its own right, and has to be pronounced. In the words *chiesa, ghiotto* and *schiava* the *h* is silent but the *i* is not. The *i* is a semiconsonant and the words are pronounced ['kjɛzɑ], ['gjottɔ], ['skjɑvɑ].

PRACTICING HARD AND SOFT *c*

The [k] should be mediopalatal and unaspirated.

Compare and practice, first speaking, then singing:

EXERCISE I

Hard Mediopalatal [k]	*Soft Prepalatal* [tʃ]
caro ['kaɾɔ]	ciarla ['tʃarla]
con ['kɔn]	ciò ['tʃɔ]
cura ['kuɾa]	ciurma ['tʃurma]
che ['kɛ]	ce ['tʃɛ]
china ['kina]	Cina ['tʃina]

EXERCISE II

canzone [kan'tsonɛ]	baciare [ba'tʃaɾɛ]
colore [kɔ'loɾɛ]	ciotola ['tʃɔtɔla]
curioso [ku'ɾjozɔ]	fanciulla [fan'tʃulla]
chetare [kɛ'taɾɛ]	lacerato [latʃɛ'ɾatɔ]
chimera [ki'mɛɾa]	cinguettio [tʃiŋgwɛt'tiːɔ]

PRACTICING HARD AND SOFT *g*

The [g] should be mediopalatal and fully voiced.
Compare and practice, first speaking, then singing:

EXERCISE I

Hard Mediopalatal [g]	*Soft Prepalatal* [dʒ]
gara ['gaɾa]	giara ['dʒaɾa]
gota ['gɔta]	gioco ['dʒɔkɔ]
gusto ['gustɔ]	giusto ['dʒustɔ]
ghetta ['getta]	getta ['dʒetta]
ghiro ['giɾɔ]	giro ['dʒiɾɔ]

EXERCISE II

gabbato [gab'batɔ]	giaccio ['dʒattʃɔ]
agone [a'gonɛ]	gioielli [dʒɔ'jɛlli]
aguzzo [a'guttsɔ]	giuramento [dʒuɾa'mentɔ]
streghe ['stregɛ]	fuggevole [fud'dʒevɔlɛ]
ghirlanda [gir'landa]	ginocchio [dʒi'nɔkkjɔ]

PRACTICING HARD AND SOFT *sc*

The [k] in the combination [sk] should be mediopalatal and unaspirated.

Compare and practice:

EXERCISE I

Hard Mediopalatal [sk]	*Soft Prepalatal* [ʃ]
scala ['skɑlɑ]	sciala ['ʃɑlɑ]
scocco ['skɔkkɔ]	sciocco ['ʃɔkkɔ]
scuro ['skuɾɔ]	sciupo ['ʃupɔ]
schema ['skɛmɑ]	scena ['ʃɛnɑ]
schivo ['skivɔ]	scivolo ['ʃivɔlɔ]

EXERCISE II

frasca ['frɑskɑ]	sciabola ['ʃɑbɔlɑ]
scongiuro [skɔn'dʒuɾɔ]	sciogliere ['ʃɔʎɛɾɛ]
scusare [sku'zɑɾɛ]	sciupare [ʃu'pɑɾɛ]
maschere ['mɑskɛɾɛ]	conoscere [kɔ'noʃɛɾɛ]
boschi ['boski]	fascino ['fɑʃinɔ]

WORDS SUCH AS *cielo, effigie, scienza*

In the following words the *i* in the syllables *cie, gie* and *scie* is silent.

cielo ['tʃɛlɔ]	sufficiente [suffi'tʃɛntɛ]	regie ['rɛdʒɛ]
cieco ['tʃɛkɔ]	effigie [ɛf'fidʒɛ]	egregie [ɛ'grɛdʒɛ]
cieca ['tʃɛkɑ]	leggiero [lɛd'dʒɛɾɔ]	scienza ['ʃɛntsɑ]
specie ['spɛtʃɛ]	messaggiero [mɛssɑd'dʒɛɾɔ]	coscienza [kɔ'ʃɛntsɑ]
camicie [kɑ'mitʃɛ]	ciliegie [tʃi'ljɛdʒɛ]	conscie ['kɔnʃɛ]
arciere [ɑr'tʃɛɾɛ]	grigie ['gridʒɛ]	

WORDS SUCH AS *Lucìa, bugìa, fruscìo*

According to the rules of *c, g* and *sc,* the *i* in words as *Lucìa, bugìa* and *fruscìo* should be silent. But it is not.

This *i* is actually syllabic and stressed and is mostly spelled with a grave accent to show that it is a stressed and long vowel, and not a diacritical mark.

The correct pronunciation is [lu'tʃi:ɑ], [bu'dʒi:ɑ], [fru'ʃi:ɔ].

The following are other words belonging to the same category:

gìa ['dʒi:ɑ] (*he was going,* poet., not to be confused with *già* ['dʒɑ] meaning *already*)

fuggìa [fud'dʒi:ɑ] (*he was escaping,* poet. for *fuggiva* [fud'dʒivɑ])

magìa [mɑ'dʒi:ɑ]

gaggìa [gɑd'dʒi:ɑ]

nostalgìa [nɔstɑl'dʒi:ɑ]

gorgheggìo [gɔrgɛd'dʒi:ɔ] (*warble,* not to be confused with *gorgheggio* [gɔr'geddʒɔ] meaning *trill, vocal exercise*)

scìa ['ʃi:ɑ]

THE PRONUNCIATION OF DOUBLE *c* AND DOUBLE *g*

When preceding a softening vowel, a double *c* and double *g* will sound like [ttʃ] and [ddʒ] respectively.

This must be stressed since in English a double *c* may be pronounced [ks], and a double *g* pronounced [gdʒ], as in the words *accent* and *suggest*.

RULE

In Italian a double *c* is pronounced [kk] or [ttʃ] and a double *g* is pronounced either [gg] or [ddʒ].

Speak, then sing:

macchia ['mɑkkjɑ]	legga ['lɛggɑ]
fiaccola ['fjɑkkɔlɑ]	fuggono ['fuggɔnɔ]
laccio ['lɑttʃɔ]	coraggio [kɔ'ɾɑddʒɔ]
acciuga [ɑt'tʃugɑ]	leggero [lɛd'dʒɛɾɔ]
uccello [ut'tʃɛllɔ]	oggetto [ɔd'dʒɛttɔ]
eccellente [ɛttʃɛl'lɛntɛ]	selvaggio [sɛl'vɑddʒɔ]
uccidere [ut'tʃidɛɾɛ]	suggerire [suddʒɛ'ɾiɾɛ]
acciuffare [ɑttʃuf'fɑɾɛ]	messaggero [mɛssɑd'dʒɛɾɔ]

8 THE PREPALATAL CONSONANTS [ɲ] AND [ʎ]

THE PREPALATAL [ɲ]

CLASSIFICATION

The consonant [ɲ] is a "nasal voiced prepalatal" (see Chart I).

DISCUSSION

The prepalatal [ɲ] occurs not only in Italian but also in French (*digne, agneau*), Spanish (*señor, puñal*) and Portuguese (*linha, companhia*). It does not occur in English.

SPELLING

In Italian the sound [ɲ] is spelled *gn*.

DIRECTIONS

To say [ɲ], the tip of the tongue is in contact with the lower front teeth, while the front of the tongue is raised and pressed against the front of the hard palate; hence the term "prepalatal." The breath streams through the nose, causing nasality.

While anchoring the tip of the tongue against the lower front teeth, say an *n* with the front of the tongue against the front of the hard palate. What will actually be said is the prepalatal [ɲ].

[ɲ] VERSUS [nj]

English-speaking persons tend to substitute the familiar [nj] (as in *onion, canyon*) for the unfamiliar prepalatal [ɲ] sound. Since there is a difference between the two, this substitution must be avoided.

The difference is that whereas the Italian [ɲ] is made with a single articulatory movement of the front, not the tip, of the tongue against the front of the hard palate, the articulation of [nj] requires two movements: the lifting of the tip of the tongue to the upper gum ridge (or teeth) for the *n,* followed by the lowering of the tip of the tongue to the lower teeth and the simultaneous raising of the front of the tongue for the semiconsonant [j]. (See Part IV, Section 3.) Obviously, the [nj] in the English *senior* and the [ɲ] in the Italian *signore* [si'ɲorɛ] sound quite different.

Furthermore, Italian has both the simple [ɲ] and the compound [nj] sounds. Sometimes they even distinguish words otherwise alike, such as *sognamo* [sɔ'ɲamɔ] (*we dream*) and *soniamo* [sɔ'njamɔ] (*we ring*).

PRACTICING THE PREPALATAL [ɲ]

Speak, then sing:

EXERCISE I

Use long vowels. The tip of the tongue should be in constant contact with the lower teeth.

[ɲiiiiɲiiiiɲiiii] [ɲuuuuɲuuuuɲuuuu]
[ɲeeeeɲeeeeɲeeee] [ɲooooɲooooɲoooo]
[ɲɛɛɛɛɲɛɛɛɛɲɛɛɛɛ] [ɲɔɔɔɔɲɔɔɔɔɲɔɔɔɔ]
[ɲɑɑɑɑɲɑɑɑɑɲɑɑɑɑ]

EXERCISE II: [ɲ] Words

gnomo ['ɲɔmɔ]
gnorri ['ɲɔrri]
pugno ['puɲɔ]
degno ['deɲɔ]
sogno ['soɲɔ]
segno ['seɲɔ]
regno ['reɲɔ]
ignaro [i'ɲɑrɔ]
ognora [ɔ'ɲorɑ]
agnello [ɑ'ɲɛllɔ]
signore [si'ɲorɛ]
sostegno [sɔ'steɲɔ]
sogghigno [sɔg'giɲɔ]
compagno [kɔm'pɑɲɔ]
montagna [mɔn'tɑɲɑ]
sognare [sɔ'ɲɑrɛ]
magnanimo [mɑ'ɲanimɔ]
agognare [ɑgɔ'ɲɑrɛ]
Don Magnifico [dɔn mɑ'ɲifikɔ]
Parpignol [pɑrpi'ɲɔl]

THE PREPALATAL [ʎ]

CLASSIFICATION

The consonant [ʎ] is a "lateral voiced prepalatal" (see Chart I).

DISCUSSION

The prepalatal [ʎ] occurs in Italian, as well as in Castillian Spanish (*calle, brillar*) and Portuguese (*bilhete, velho*). It does not occur in English.

SPELLING

In Italian the sound [ʎ] is spelled *gli, glie, glia, glio* or *gliu.*

DIRECTIONS

To say [ʎ] the tip of the tongue is in contact with the lower teeth, while the front of the tongue is raised and pressed against the front of the hard palate. The air streams out laterally over the sides of the tongue.

Anchor the tip of the tongue against the lower front teeth. Articulate an *l* with the front of the tongue against the front of the hard palate. You will actually be saying the prepalatal [ʎ].

[ʎ] Versus [lj]

English-speaking persons tend to substitute the familiar [lj] (as in *valiant, filial*) for the unfamiliar prepalatal [ʎ] sound. This must be avoided, since the difference between [ʎ] and [lj] is considerable.

The difference is that, whereas the [ʎ] is made with a single articulatory movement of the front, not the tip, of the tongue against the front of the hard palate, the articulation of [lj] requires two distinct movements: the lifting of the tip of the tongue to the upper gum ridge (or teeth) for the *l,* followed by the lowering of the tip of the tongue to the lower teeth and the simultaneous raising of the front of the tongue for the semiconsonant [j]. Obviously, the [lj] in the English *million* and the [ʎ] in the Italian *miglio* ['miʎɔ] will sound quite different.

Furthermore, Italian has both the simple [ʎ] and the compound [lj] sounds. Sometimes they even distinguish otherwise identical words, such as *vogliamo* [vɔ'ʎɑmɔ] (*we want*) and *voliamo* [vɔ'ljɑmɔ] (*we fly*), or *ammagliare* [ɑmmɑ'ʎɑrɛ] (*to tie*) and *ammaliare* [ɑmmɑ'ljɑrɛ] (*to bewitch*).

Practicing The Prepalatal [ʎ]

Speak, then sing:

EXERCISE I

Use long vowels and keep the tip of the tongue in constant contact with the lower teeth.

[ʎiiiiʎiiiiʎiiii] [ʎuuuuʎuuuuʎuuuu]
[ʎeeeeʎeeeeʎeeee] [ʎooooʎooooʎoooo]
[ʎɛɛɛɛʎɛɛɛɛʎɛɛɛɛ] [ʎɔɔɔɔʎɔɔɔɔʎɔɔɔɔ]
[ʎɑɑɑɑʎɑɑɑɑʎɑɑɑɑ]

EXERCISE II: [ʎ] Words

gli ['ʎi]
glielo ['ʎɛlɔ]
gliela ['ʎɛlɑ]
egli ['eʎi]
figlio ['fiʎɔ]
giglio ['dʒiʎɔ]
ciglio ['tʃiʎɔ]
meglio ['mɛʎɔ]

soglia ['sɔʎɑ]
doglie ['dɔʎɛ]
moglie ['moʎɛ]
foglia ['fɔʎɑ]
pariglia [pɑ'ɾiʎɑ]
consiglio [kɔn'siʎɔ]
imbroglio [im'brɔʎɔ]
vegliardo [vɛ'ʎardɔ]

famiglia [fɑ'miʎɑ]
battaglia [bɑt'tɑʎɑ]
doglioso [dɔ'ʎozɔ]
migliora [mi'ʎoɾɑ]
smagliante [zmɑ'ʎɑntɛ]
Siviglia [si'viʎɑ]
Pagliacci [pɑ'ʎɑttʃi]
Guglielmo [gu'ʎɛlmɔ]

REMARK ON THE PRONUNCIATION OF *gli*

The letters *gli* are not always pronounced [ʎ] in Italian. In certain instances they are pronounced [gli], as in the English word *glee*.

This is the case whenever the sequence *gli* is:

a) initial, except for the pronouns *gli, glielo, gliela, glieli, gliele, gliene,*

EXAMPLE: glicine ['glitʃinɛ]

b) preceded by the letter *n*,

EXAMPLE: Anglia ['ɑŋgljɑ]

c) part of the words *negligere* [nɛ'glidʒɛɾɛ], *negligenza* [nɛgli'dʒɛntsɑ], *negligente* [nɛgli'dʒɛntɛ], etc.

In all other instances *gli* is pronounced [ʎ].

9 THE PRONUNCIATION OF THE LETTERS *h, j, k, q, w, x, y*

The Letter *h*

The letter *h* is always silent in Italian.

In addition to being inserted between *c, g* or *sc* and the softening vowels *e* or *i* so as to harden these consonants, it is found as the silent initial of the following four forms of the verb *avere* [ɑ'veɾɛ]: *ho* ['ɔ], *hai* ['ɑːĭ], *ha* ['ɑ], *hanno* ['ɑnnɔ].

It may also be found following a vowel, as in the interjections *ah* ['ɑ], *eh* ['ɛ], *oh* ['ɔ], *ahi* ['ɑːĭ], *ohi* ['ɔːĭ], *ahimè* [ɑːĭ'mɛ], *ohimè* [ɔːĭ'mɛ]. In these instances it prolongs the vowel.

The Letter *j*

The letter *j* is not used in modern Italian spelling. It may be found, however, in older books and vocal scores where it once symbolized the semiconsonant [j], to distinguish it from the vowel [i]. Thus one may come across the spelling *muojo* for *muoio* ['mwɔjɔ] or *gajo* for *gaio* ['gɑjɔ] or *boja* for *boia* ['bɔjɑ].

The Letter *k*

There is no letter *k* in the Italian alphabet. A *k* occurs only in foreign words, such as *kimono* [ki'mɔnɔ] or *whisky* ['wiski]. It is pronounced [k].

The Letter *q*

The letter *q,* always followed by *u,* is pronounced [k]. The *u* is invariably a semiconsonant, pronounced [w]—that is, *quando* ['kwɑndɔ], *qui* ['kwi].

The sequence *cq* in such words as *acqua* ['ɑkkwɑ], *nacque* ['nɑkkwɛ] stands for double [k].

The Letter *w*

The letter *w* is not found in the Italian alphabet, and occurs only in foreign words. It should be pronounced according to the language in which it appears. The *w* in *La fanciulla del West* should have the English [w] sound, but the *w* in *La Wally* should have the German [v] sound.

The Letter *x*

The letter *x* is not found in the Italian alphabet, and occurs only in foreign words. The word *Xeres* (*Falstaff,* Act I) is pronounced ['kɛrɛs] to approximate the Spanish pronunciation.

The Letter *y*

y is also not found in the Italian alphabet, and occurs only in foreign words, where it is pronounced according to the language in which it appears. For instance, in the words *Butterfly* and *Yankee,* it is pronounced as in English.

Part IV

THE SEMICONSONANTS

OUTLINE

Italian and English share the same two "semiconsonants," the [j] as in the Italian *ieri* ['jɛri] and as in *you,* and the [w] as in the Italian *uomo* ['wɔmɔ] and as in *warm* (see Chart I).

1 DEFINITION AND DISCUSSION

A semiconsonant is a voiced sound, uttered neither with as open a breath passage as required by a vowel, nor with the constriction characteristic of a consonant. It partakes of the characteristics of both vowels and consonants. Hence the term "semiconsonant."

In Italian the semiconsonants are shorter than the English ones and spoken with more energy and intensity.

2 CHARACTERISTICS

Semiconsonants are short and unstressed by nature. They are invariably followed by a long vowel that bears the stress within the syllable, as in *piuma* ['pjumɑ] or *guardare* [gwar'dɑrɛ]. It often, though not necessarily, also bears the stress within the word.

3 THE SEMICONSONANT [j]

SPELLING

In Italian the semiconsonant [j] is spelled with the letter *i.* It was formerly spelled with a *j.*

DIRECTIONS

The semiconsonant [j] is uttered with a tongue and lip position similar to that of the first front vowel [i]. Accordingly the [j] also requires fronting of the tongue and spreading of the lips, even more markedly in Italian than in English, so as to achieve the stronger friction characteristic of the Italian semiconsonant.

The short, sharp [j] and the long vowel following it form one syllable and should be made to share a single stress and pulse.

Some English-speaking singers tend to weaken and lengthen a [j] to the point of splitting a single syllable such as [ˈjɛ] into the two syllables [iˈɛ]. This must be avoided.

EXERCISE

Speak, then sing, concentrating on a short, intense [j] and greatly sustaining the vowel that follows:

ieri [ˈjɛɾi]	aiuto [ɑˈjutɔ]	cavaliere [kɑvɑˈljɛɾɛ]
noia [ˈnɔjɑ]	fioraia [fjɔˈɾɑjɑ]	gondoliere [gɔndɔˈljɛɾɛ]
siamo [ˈsjɑmɔ]	preghiera [prɛˈgjɛɾɑ]	barcaiolo [bɑrkɑˈjɔlɔ]
miele [ˈmjɛlɛ]	bicchiere [bikˈkjɛɾɛ]	Jago [ˈjɑgɔ]
fiele [ˈfjɛlɛ]	sembiante [sɛmˈbjɑntɛ]	Fiora [ˈfjoɾɑ]
gabbia [ˈgɑbbjɑ]	cantiamo [ˈkɑnˈtjɑmɔ]	Fiammetta [fjɑmˈmettɑ]
specchio [ˈspɛkkjɔ]	chiudere [ˈkjudɛɾɛ]	Notaio [noˈtɑjɔ]
occhio [ˈɔkkjɔ]	cameriere [kɑmɛˈɾjɛɾɛ]	Carceriere [kɑrtʃɛˈɾjɛɾɛ]

4 THE SEMICONSONANT [w]

SPELLING

The semiconsonant [w] is spelled with the letter *u*.

DIRECTIONS

The [w] is uttered with a tongue and lip position similar to that of the first back vowel [u]. It requires backing of the tongue and rounding of the lips, even more markedly in Italian than in English, so as to achieve the stronger friction required by the Italian sound.

The short, energetic [w] and the long vowel that follows pertain to the same syllable and should be made to share a single stress and pulse.

Some English-speaking singers tend to weaken and lengthen a [w] to the point of making a single syllable such as [ˈwɑ] sound like the two syllables [uˈɑ]. This must be avoided.

EXERCISE

Speak, then sing, with a short, sharp [w] and greatly sustaining the vowel that follows:

nuovo [ˈnwɔvɔ]	guerra [ˈgwɛrrɑ]
fuoco [ˈfwɔkɔ]	sguardo [ˈzgwɑrdɔ]
cuore [ˈkwɔɾɛ]	duolo [ˈdwɔlɔ]
stuolo [ˈstwɔlɔ]	guanciale [gwɑnˈtʃɑlɛ]
fuori [ˈfwɔɾi]	guerriero [gwɛrˈrjɛɾɔ]
uomo [ˈwɔmɔ]	languire [lɑŋˈgwiɾɛ]

guizzare [gwit'tsaɾɛ]
guindolo ['gwindɔlɔ]
tranquillo [traŋ'kwillɔ]
qualità [kwali'ta]
liquore [li'kwoɾɛ]
guarire [gwa'ɾiɾɛ]
eguale [ɛ'gwalɛ]
Buoso ['bwɔzɔ]
Pasquale [pa'skwalɛ]
Suor Angelica [ˌswɔɾan'dʒɛlika]
Inquisitore [iŋkwizi'toɾɛ]
Guardiano [gwar'djanɔ]

5 THE THREE PHONETIC VALUES OF THE LETTER *i* AND THE TWO PHONETIC VALUES OF THE LETTER *u*

In discussing the Italian vowels in Part I, it was stated that as far as vowels are concerned the letters *i* and *u* are phonetic, and are always pronounced [i] and [u].

However, from the standpoint of the Italian language as a whole the letters *i* and *u* are not phonetic.

The *i* may stand (1) for the first front vowel [i] as in *fidi* ['fidi], (2) it may be silent as in *bacio* ['batʃɔ] and (3) it may identify the semiconsonant [j] as in *fiore* ['fjoɾɛ].

The *u* may stand either (1) for the first back vowel [u] as in *lume* ['lumɛ] or (2) for the semiconsonant [w] as in *guardie* ['gwardjɛ].

The small chart on the pronunciation of *c, g* and *sc* (Part III, Section 7) shows when *i* is silent. But one still needs to know when *i* and *u* stand for a semiconsonant and not a vowel.

6 RULE FOR IDENTIFYING SEMICONSONANTS

In a polysyllable, an *i* or *u* is a semiconsonant whenever it shares one note with a vowel that follows.

This rule is only valid for singing (see Appendix III).

However, the following verb forms are exceptions to this rule; they are all 3rd Person Pl. of the Present Indicative or Subjunctive: *siano* ['siːănɔ] (archaic *sieno* ['siːĕnɔ]), *stiano* ['stiːănɔ], *diano* ['diːănɔ], *fiano* ['fiːănɔ], *spiano* ['spiːănɔ], *inviano* [in'viːănɔ], *avviano* [av'viːănɔ].

EXAMPLES

Speak, then sing:

Pagliacci, Act I

Pagliacci, Prologue *

[son traŋ-′kwil-lăeː ′ljɛ - ta]

La Bohème, Act I

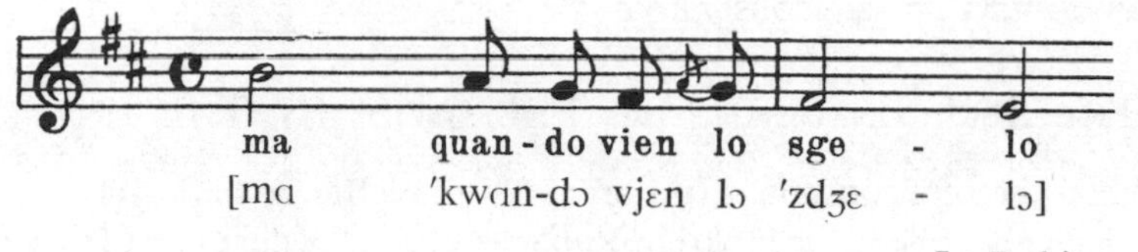

La Bohème, Act I

siam and *vien* are apocopated forms of *siamo* [′sjamɔ] and *viene* [′vjɛnɛ] and are polysyllables.

7 MORE ON THE SEMICONSONANTS

(A) PRONUNCIATION OF *qu* + VOWEL AND *gu* + VOWEL

In the letter sequences *qu + vowel* and *gu + vowel* the *u* identifies the semiconsonant [w]. This should be emphasized because in French, German and some Italian dialects, these letters are pronounced in various ways, all different from standard Italian.

In standard Italian, *qu + vowel* and *gu + vowel* always sound like [kw] and [gw].

questo [′kwestɔ]	guida [′gwida]
quello [′kwellɔ]	guisa [′gwiza]
quale [′kwalɛ]	guardie [′gwardjɛ]
quindi [′kwindi]	guancia [′gwantʃa]
squillo [′skwillɔ]	guardinfante [gwardin′fantɛ]
tranquillo [traŋ′kwillɔ]	languente [laŋ′gwɛntɛ]

* See footnote, p. 37.

(B) THE SEMICONSONANT [j] FOLLOWED BY THE LETTER *e*

When the semiconsonant [j] precedes the letter *e,* the *e* has an open sound. The sequence [je] does not occur in Italian, but [jɛ] occurs very frequently.

chiesa ['kjɛzɑ]	indietro [in'djɛtrɔ]
diedi ['djɛdi]	cimiero [tʃi'mjɛrɔ]
lieto ['ljɛtɔ]	forestiero [fɔrɛ'stjɛrɔ]
mieto ['mjɛtɔ]	giardiniere [dʒɑrdi'njɛrɛ]

REMARK

Such words as *biglietto* and *foglietto* have a close [e] and may look as if they contained the sequence [je]. But this is not so because *gli* is the spelling of the simple prepalatal [ʎ].

Thus the phonetic transcription of these words is [bi'ʎettɔ], [fɔ'ʎettɔ] and they contain no semiconsonant.

(C) THE SEMICONSONANT [w] FOLLOWED BY THE LETTER *o*

When the semiconsonant [w] precedes the letter *o,* the *o* has an open sound. There is no sequence [wo] in Italian, but [wɔ] occurs most frequently.

buono ['bwɔnɔ]	uomini ['wɔmini]
suolo ['swɔlɔ]	muovere ['mwɔvɛrɛ]
luogo ['lwɔgɔ]	frastuono [frɑ'stwɔnɔ]
stuolo ['stwɔlɔ]	galantuomo [gɑlɑn'twɔmɔ]

(D) THREE-LETTER WORDS WITH AND WITHOUT SEMICONSONANT

Italian has a wealth of short words consisting of an initial consonant (sometimes two) followed by the letter *i* or *u* and ending with another vowel. These words are often misstressed by non-Italians.

A certain amount of confusion is created because in some of these words the *i* or *u* is a semiconsonant, which causes the stress to fall on the final vowel. In others the *i* or *u* is a full vowel and carries the stress of the word.

THREE-LETTER WORDS CONTAINING A SEMICONSONANT

Such words as the following contain a semiconsonant and are stressed on the final vowel.

diè ['djɛ]	può ['pwɔ]
piè ['pjɛ]	qui ['kwi]
più ['pju]	qua ['kwɑ]
Liù ['lju]	

That the *i* or *u* is a semiconsonant is indicated either by the grave accent on the final vowel or by the spelling *qu + vowel.*

EXAMPLES

Speak, then sing:

Turandot, Act I

Tosca, Act I

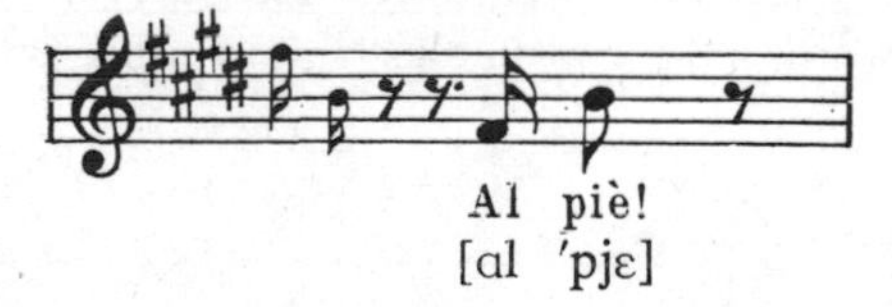

La Bohème, Act II

Pagliacci, Prologue

Madama Butterfly, Act I

Three-Letter Words Without Semiconsonant

Such words as the ones listed below, with neither a grave accent on the final vowel nor an initial *q,* contain no semiconsonant and must be stressed on the vowel before last, the *i* or *u.*

Practice these often mispronounced words distinctly sustaining the *i* or *u* (as symbolized by [ː]) and sounding a very short, though unweakened, final vowel (as symbolized by [˘]).

mio, mia, mie [ˈmiːɔ̆] [ˈmiːɑ̆] [ˈmiːɛ̆]
tuo, tua, tue [ˈtuːɔ̆] [ˈtuːɑ̆] [ˈtuːɛ̆]
suo, sua, sue [ˈsuːɔ̆] [ˈsuɑ̆] [ˈsuːɛ̆]
dia, fia, sia, stia (v.) [ˈdiːɑ̆] [fiːɑ̆] [siːɑ̆] [ˈstiːɑ̆]
zio, zia, zii, zie [ˈtsiːɔ̆] [ˈtsiːɑ̆] [ˈtsiːĭ] [ˈtsiːɛ̆]
pio, pia, pii, pie [ˈpiːɔ̆] [ˈpiːɑ̆] [piːĭ] [ˈpiːɛ̆]
rio, ria, rii, rie (adj.) [ˈriːɔ̆] [ˈriːɑ̆] [riːĭ] [ˈriːɛ̆]
rio, rii (n.) [ˈriːɔ̆] [ˈriːĭ]
spio, spii, spia (v.) [ˈspiːɔ̆] [ˈspiːĭ] [ˈspiːɑ̆]
spia, spie (n.) [ˈspiːɑ̆] [ˈspiːɛ̆]
via, vie [ˈviːɑ̆] [ˈviːɛ̆]
Dio [ˈdiːɔ̆]
fio [ˈfiːɔ̆]
brio [ˈbriːɔ̆]
trio [ˈtriːɔ̆]
pria (poet. for *prima*) [ˈpriːɑ̆]
sui [ˈsuːĭ]
fui [ˈfuːĭ]
cui [ˈkuːĭ]
lui [ˈluːĭ]
due [ˈduːɛ̆]
bue [ˈbuːɛ̆]

Actually, in poetry these words may be used either as monosyllables or as dissyllables (words of two syllables), depending on their position in the verse.

EXAMPLES

"Amarilli, mia bella" by Caccini

"Amarilli, mia bella" by Caccini

When used as dissyllables and set on two notes (as in the second example), these words present no problem to the singer. But, when used as monosyllables and set on a single note (first example), they contain a falling diphthong. (See Part V, Section 1.)

Avoid the common error of giving half of the note to the first vowel and half to the second. Also, avoid the more serious error of stressing and prolonging the final vowel and reducing the preceding *i* or *u* to a semiconsonant.

The word is neither ['mi-'ɑ] nor ['mjɑ] but ['mi:ă].

EXAMPLES

Speak, then sing:

Falstaff, Act II

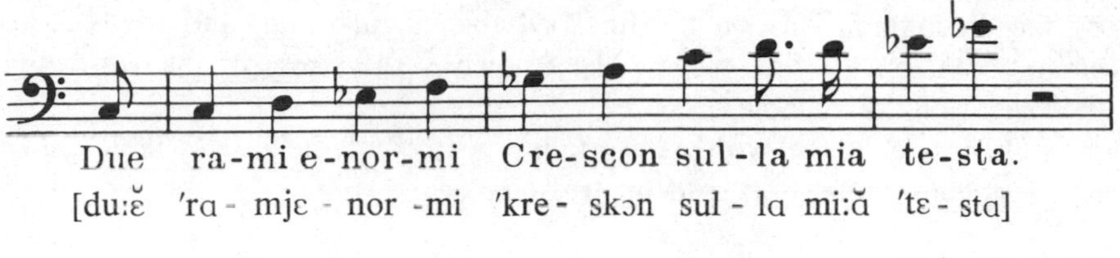

Falstaff, Act II

Falstaff, Act III

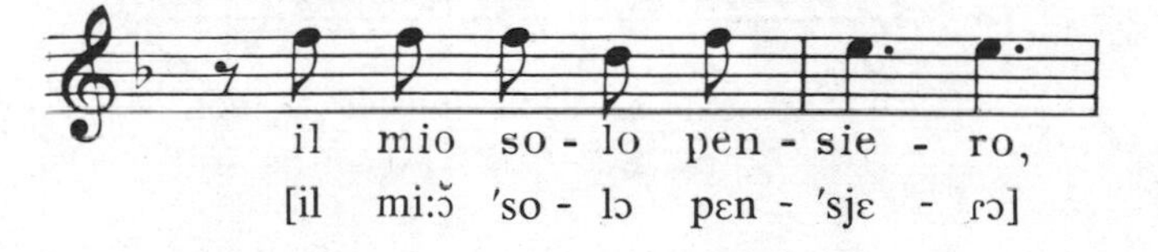

Tosca, Act I

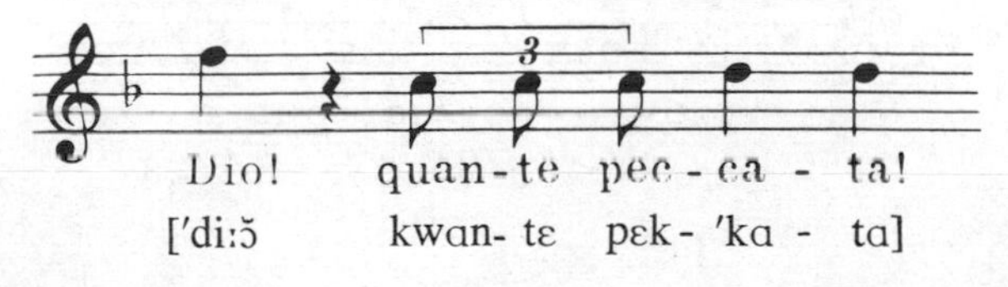

Tosca, Act I

(E) Polysyllables Ending With *-io, -ia, -ie*

In Italian many polysyllables end with the letters *io, ia* or *ie*. These polysyllables are easily misstressed by non-Italians.

The confusion occurs because in some of these polysyllables the *i* is stressed and sustained, as in *natio* [nɑ'tiːɔ̆] or *bramosia* [brɑmɔ'ziːɑ̆], but in others the final vowel is prolonged, since the *i* is a semiconsonant, as in *boia* ['bɔjɑ] or *notaio* [nɔ'tɑjɔ].

The problem is how to enable a singer to stress such words properly and to give the letter *i* its correct value so that baritones in *La Traviata,* for instance, will not sing [nɑ'tjɔ] for [nɑ'tiːɔ̆]. The solution is as follows.

RULE

If the stress of the word, as revealed by the rhythm of the music or by the dictionary, falls on the final syllable *io, ia* or *ie,* and there is no grave accent on the final vowel, the *i* receives the stress of the word and the length of the syllable.

Otherwise, if the word stress falls on any but the last syllable, the *i* is a semiconsonant short and unstressed.

EXAMPLES

Speak, then sing:

(a) THE *i* OF THE ENDING IS STRESSED AND LONG because the final syllable falls on a strong beat and there is no grave accent on the final vowel.

La Traviata, Act II

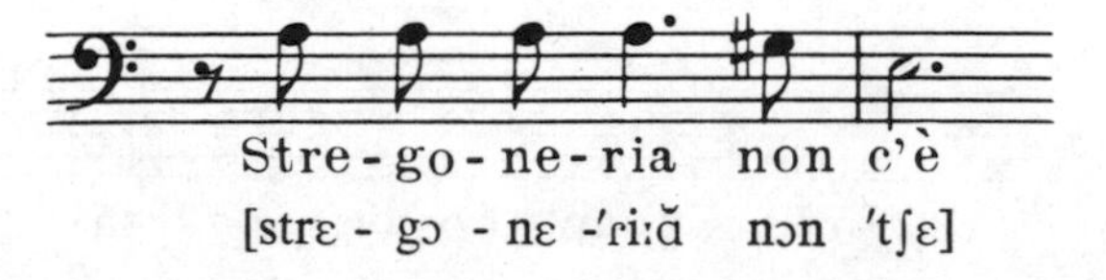

Falstaff, Act II

La Bohème, Act II

Tosca, Act II

In the first and third examples, sustain the *i* on all notes (including the grace notes) and add the final *o* or *a* at the very end of the last note.

(b) THE *i* OF THE ENDING IS A SEMICONSONANT, UNSTRESSED AND SHORT because the rhythm reveals that the final syllable is unstressed. The final vowel should be sustained.

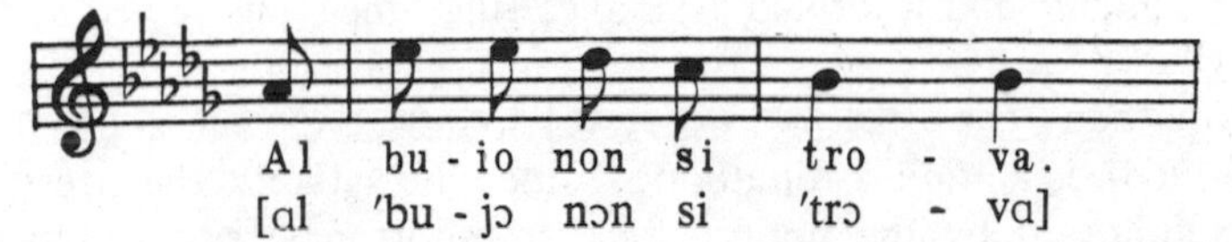

La Bohème, Act I

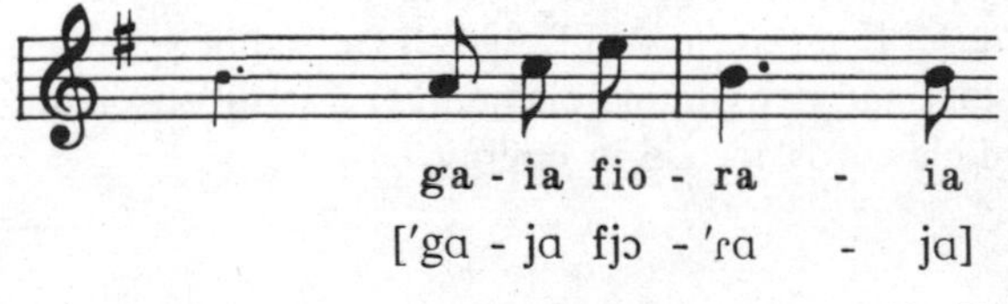

La Bohème, Act II

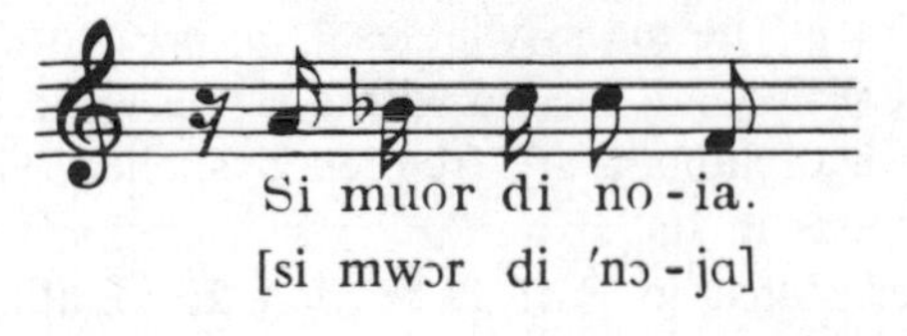

Il barbiere di Siviglia, Act I

Part V

DIPHTHONGS AND TRIPHTHONGS

1 THE DIPHTHONGS

OUTLINE

In common with English, Italian has two kinds of diphthongs, "falling diphthongs" as in the Italian *aura* [ˈɑːŭɾɑ] and as in *house,* and "rising" or "semiconsonantal diphthongs" as in the Italian *fiore* [ˈfjoɾɛ] and as in *yarn.*

DEFINITION AND DISCUSSION

A diphthong is a sequence either of two vowel sounds or of a semiconsonant and a vowel uttered in the same syllable.

One of the two elements of a diphthong bears the length and stress within the syllable and is termed "syllabic," the other, unstressed and short, is "nonsyllabic."

A diphthong consisting of two vowel sounds, as in *lauro* [ˈlɑːŭɾɔ] and *feudo* [ˈfɛːŭdɔ], is a "falling diphthong," since the syllabic, the stressed long vowel, is followed by the nonsyllabic, the short unstressed vowel. This causes a falling off in energy.

Conversely, a diphthong consisting of a semiconsonant followed by a vowel, as in *lieto* [ˈljɛtɔ] or *luogo* [ˈlwɔgɔ], is a "semiconsonantal" or "rising diphthong," since the nonsyllabic element, the semiconsonant, precedes the syllabic one. This causes a rise in energy.

SPELLING

The English words *aisle, eight, dough* contain the English falling diphthongs [aĭ], [eĭ], [oŭ]. The monosyllables *I, a, no* contain the same three diphthongs. But here they are spelled with a single vowel letter. In English, the two sounds of a diphthong are frequently spelled with a single letter, but this never happens in Italian.

In English, as stated in Part I, Section 2, diphthongs prevail over monophthongs, while in Italian the opposite is true. Because of this frequency of English diphthongs, English-speaking singers tend also to diphthongize those Italian vowels which are monophthongal. But knowing that Italian diphthongs are spelled phonetically with two vowel letters should help to overcome such a tendency.

(A) Falling Diphthongs

Italian falling diphthongs consist of a long vowel stressed within the syllable (and often though not necessarily stressed within the word), followed by an unstressed short *i* or *u*.

Practicing Falling Diphthongs

The syllabic in an Italian falling diphthong is longer than the syllabic in an English falling diphthong.

Speak, then sing, giving the syllabic almost the entire length of the syllable or note value (as symbolized by [:]) and sounding a very short nonsyllabic *i* or *u* (as symbolized by [˘]).

Move energetically from the one to the other without intermediate glides.

Though very short, the *i* should not sound like the [ɪ] in the English diphthong [aɪ̆] as in *might,* but it should be a truly Italian high first front vowel [i]. Similary, the short *u* should not sound like the [ʊ] in the English diphthong [ɑʊ̆] as in *house,* but should be an energetic Italian high first back vowel [u].

EXERCISE I

ahi ['ɑ:ĭ]	lui ['lu:ĭ]	aurora [ɑ:ŭ'ɾɔɾɑ]
mai ['mɑ:ĭ]	cui ['ku:ĭ]	feudale [fɛ:ŭ'dɑlɛ]
ehi ['ɛ:ĭ]	aura ['ɑ:ŭɾɑ]	laudato [lɑ:ŭ'dɑtɔ]
lei ['lɛ:ĭ]	flauto ['flɑ:ŭtɔ]	Claudio ['k̟lɑ:ŭdjɔ]
ohi ['ɔ:ĭ]	cauto ['kɑ:ŭtɔ]	Laura ['lɑ:ŭɾɑ]
poi ['pɔ:ĭ]	lauro ['lɑ:ŭɾɔ]	Lauretta [lɑ:ŭ'ɾettɑ]
noi ['no:ĭ]	feudo ['fɛ:ŭdɔ]	Euridice [ɛ:ŭɾi'ditʃɛ]
voi ['vo:ĭ]	ahimè [ɑ:ĭ'mɛ]	Raimondo [rɑ:ĭ'mondɔ]

EXERCISE II

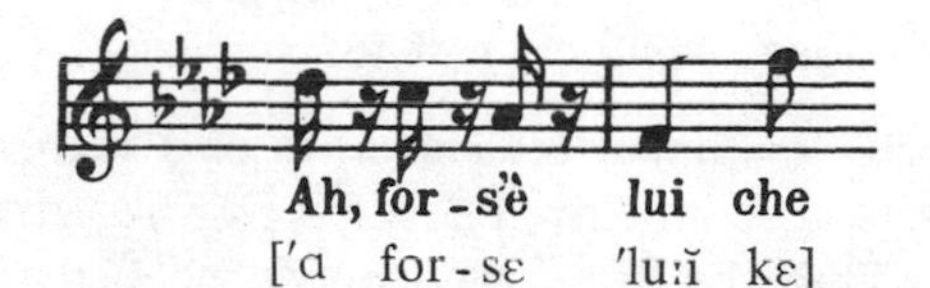

La Traviata, Act I

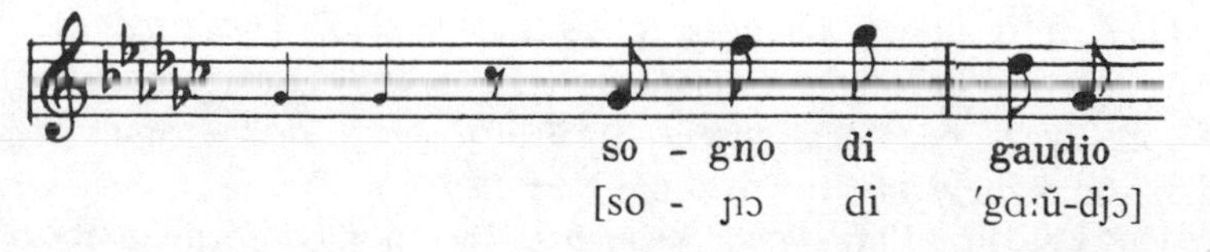

Aida, Act IV

Falstaff, Act II

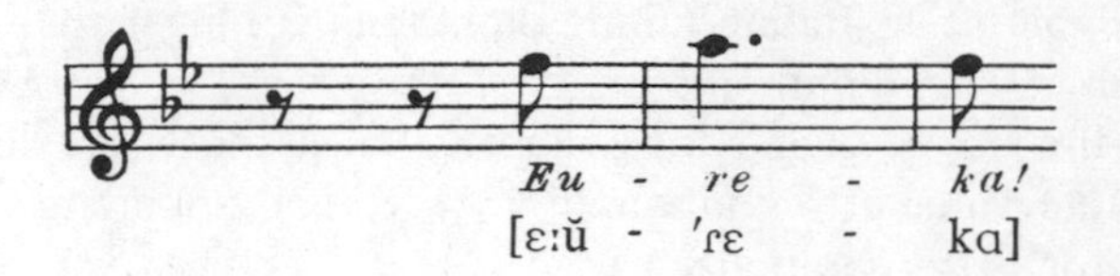

La Bohème, Act I

When a falling diphthong must be sung on more than one note, sustain the syllabic on all notes and add the nonsyllabic short *i* or *u* at the very end of the last note.

Il barbiere di Siviglia, Act I

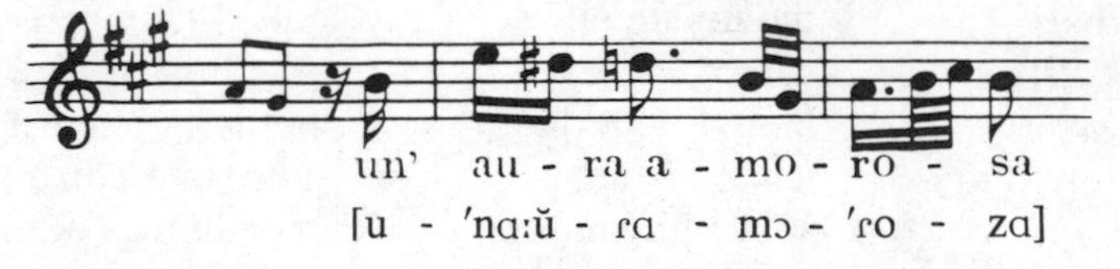

Così fan tutte, Act II

EXERCISE III: Falling Diphthongs of the Imperfect Indicative

In Italian poetry the imperfect indicative of a verb of the second and third conjugations (whose infinitive ends in *ere* or *ire*) drops the consonant *v* from its ending. Thus the two vowels previously separated by the *v* become contiguous and in lyric diction they mostly (though not necessarily) share the same note.

Godeva [gɔˈdevɑ] changes to *godea* [gɔˈdeːɑ̆] (*he used to enjoy*), *scendevano* [ʃɛnˈdevɑnɔ] to *scendeano* [ʃɛnˈdeːɑ̆nɔ] (*they descended*), *moriva* [mɔˈɾivɑ] becomes *moria* [mɔˈɾiːɑ̆] (*he died*) and *fuggivano* [fudˈdʒivɑnɔ] *fuggiano* [fudˈdʒiːɑ̆nɔ] *they fled*.)

This [ˈeːɑ̆] or [ˈiːɑ̆] vowel sequence does not conform to the normal pattern of Italian falling diphthongs (syllabic followed by nonsyllabic *i* or *u*). Nevertheless, since the *e* or *i* is stressed in the complete verb form, it is also stressed and syllabic in its poetic form. Thus we have a falling diphthong.

Speak, then sing, sustaining the syllabic and sounding the nonsyllabic *a* at the very end of the note:

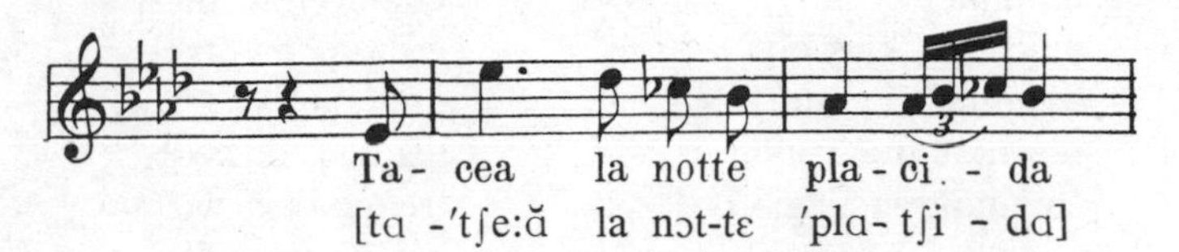

Il Trovatore, Act I

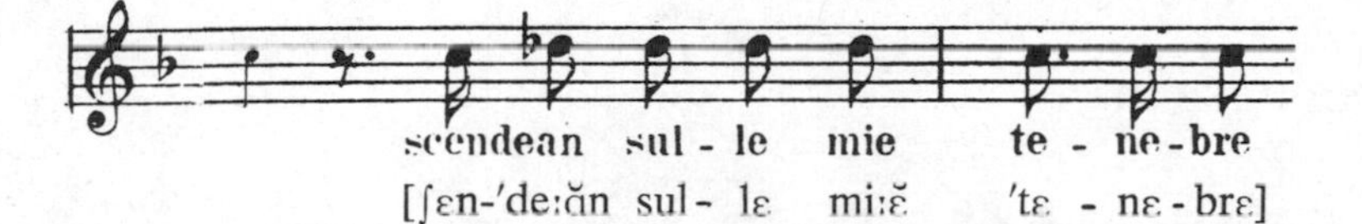

Otello, Act I

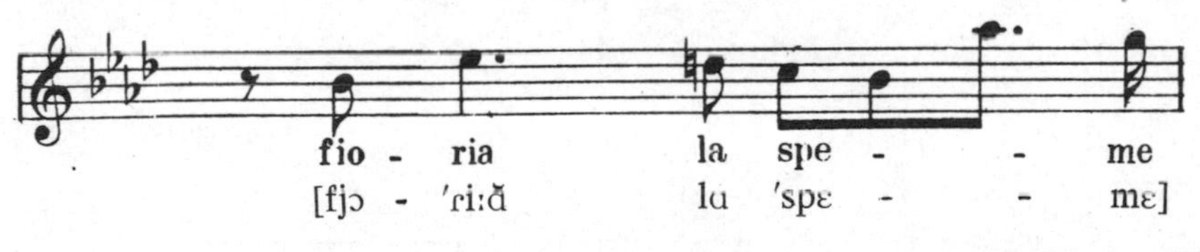

Otello, Act III

When the diphthong is sung on more than one note, sustain the syllabic on all the notes and add the *a* at the very end of the last note.

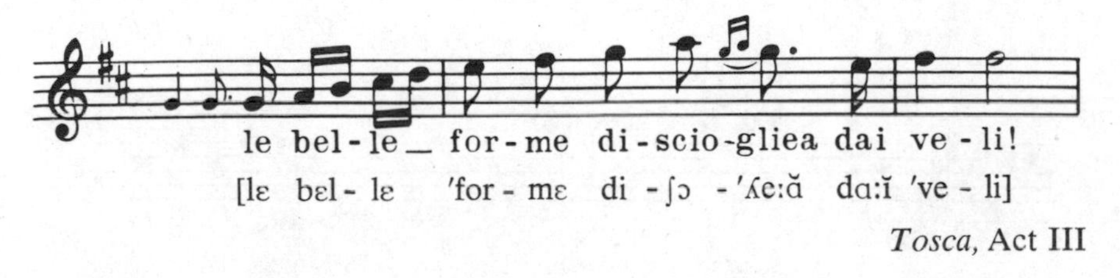

Tosca, Act III

(B) Rising Diphthongs

Rising, semiconsonantal diphthongs consist of a semiconsonant [j] or [w] followed by a long syllabic vowel bearing the stress of the syllable, and often of the word also.

Practicing Rising Diphthongs

For words with rising, semiconsonantal diphthongs see Part IV.

Practice the following, concentrating on strong short semiconsonants and sustained syllabic vowels.

EXERCISE I

chioma [ˈkjɔmɑ]
chiostro [ˈkjɔstrɔ]
fiamma [ˈfjɑmmɑ]
mestiere [mɛˈstjɛɾɛ]
singhiozzo [siŋˈgjottsɔ]
fierezza [fjɛˈɾettsɑ]
carrettiere [kɑrrɛtˈtjɛɾɛ]
giarrettiera [dʒɑrrɛtˈtjɛɾɑ]

guanto [ˈgwɑntɔ]
guizzo [ˈgwittsɔ]
quercia [ˈkwɛrtʃɑ]
acqua [ˈɑkkwɑ]
tregua [ˈtrɛgwɑ]
squillo [ˈsqwillɔ]
querela [kwɛˈɾɛlɑ]
guarire [gwɑˈɾiɾɛ]

EXERCISE II

La Bohème, Act II

Tosca, Act II

Tosca, Act I

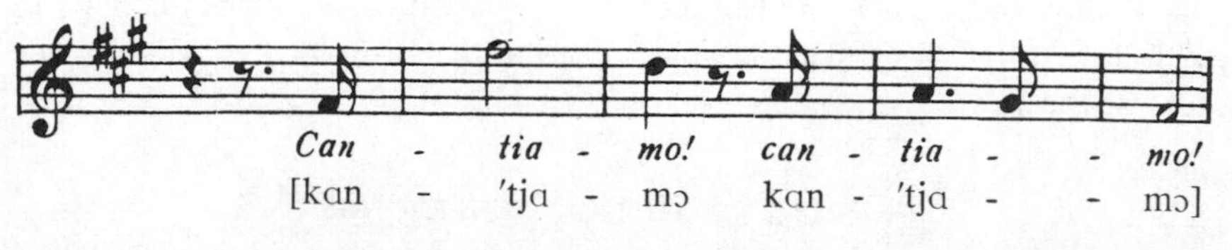

Otello, Act IV

2 THE TRIPHTHONGS

A triphthong is a sequence of either three vowel sounds, of one semiconsonant and two vowel sounds or of two semiconsonants and one vowel sound, uttered in the same syllable. In lyric diction they share the same note.

English triphthongs consist of three vowel sounds, as in *fire* [aĭə̆], *flower* [ɑʊ̆ə̆].

Conversely, Italian triphthongs are semiconsonantal, formed mostly by a rising diphthong to which a final *i* is added.

Practicing Triphthongs

EXERCISE I

Practice the following words, sustaining the syllabic and sounding a very short semiconsonant and final vowel.

miei [ˈmjɛːĭ]	guai [ˈgwɑːĭ]
tuoi [ˈtwɔːĭ]	quai [ˈkwɑːĭ] (poet. for *quali*)
suoi [ˈswɔːĭ]	quei [ˈkweːĭ]
puoi [ˈpwɔːĭ]	studiai [stuˈdjɑːĭ]
vuoi [ˈvwɔːĭ]	arrabbiai [ɑrrɑbˈbjɑːĭ]
buoi [ˈbwɔːĭ]	invidiai [inviˈdjɑːĭ]

EXERCISE II

Less frequent are the Italian triphthongs consisting of two semiconsonants followed by a vowel. Here also the syllabic should be greatly sustained.

quiete [ˈkwjɛtɛ]	requie [ˈrɛkwjɛ]	languiamo [lɑŋˈgwjɑmɔ]
quieto [ˈkwjɛtɔ]	seguiamo [sɛˈgwjɑmɔ]	languiate [lɑŋˈgwjɑtɛ]
aiuola [ɑˈjwɔlɑ]	seguiate [sɛˈgwjɑtɛ]	

EXERCISE III

In the following examples so prolong the syllabic as to give it the almost entire length of the note value. The semiconsonant and the final *i* are vigorous but extremely short.

La Traviata, Act I

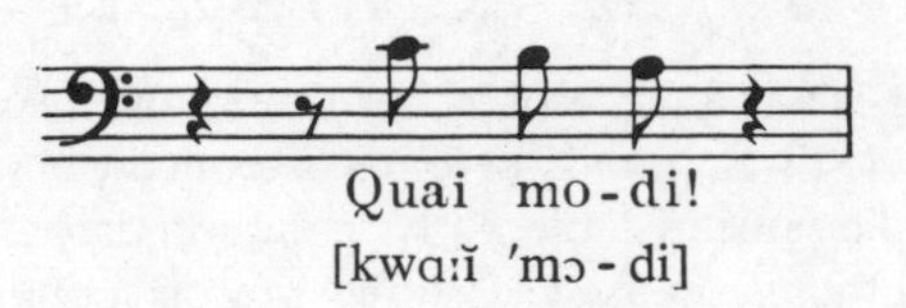

La Traviata, Act II

Aida, Act II

La Bohème, Act III

Otello, Act I

When a triphthong must be sung on more than one note, sustain the syllabic on all the notes and add the final *i* at the very end of the last note.

Le nozze di Figaro, Act I

Aida, Act II

Aida, Act III

REMARK

Non-Italians easily confuse the triphthong *vuoi* ['vwɔːĭ] (*you want,* form of the verb *volere* [vɔ'lerɛ], *to want*) with the diphthong *voi* ['voːĭ] (*you,* personal pronoun).

This is also true of the triphthong *puoi* ['pwɔːĭ] (*you can,* form of the verb *potere* [pɔ'terɛ], *to be able*), and the diphthong *poi* ['pɔːĭ] (*then,* adverb).

Practice these words until you know them well.

Part VI

SYLLABIFICATION

In Italian lyric diction, the oral syllabification corresponds to the written syllable division of words in conventional spelling. A singer, to sing a speech sound on the pitch to which it belongs, need only follow what is printed. This may not always be as easy as it appears.

English-speaking vocalists should concentrate on Italian single consonants between vowels. Unlike those in English, they are extremely short and they invariably belong syllabically to the vowel which follows and are sung on its pitch.

This rule applies to all consonants (including the *l, m* and *n* which some singers tend to anticipate and linger upon) and applies to all words regardless of their origin and grammatical combination.

The syllabification of the compound word *disonorato* [dizɔnɔ'ɾatɔ] (*dishonored*) is *di-so-no-ra-to* in spelling, speaking and singing, even though it combines the prefix *dis* and the verb form *onorato.*

Similarly, *inaudito* [inɑːŭ'ditɔ] (*unheard*), originating from the prefix *in* and the verb form *audito,* is syllabified and sung as *i-nau-di-to, inebriato* [inɛbri'ɑtɔ] (*inebriated*) as *i-ne-bri-a-to, malaugurio* [mɑlɑːŭ'guɾjɔ] (*ill omen*) as *ma-lau-gu-rio.*

The fact that the syllabification ignores the origin of compound words proves that in Italian the syllable is stronger than the word and transcends its boundaries.

In fact, the syllable so outweighs the word that when a consonant-final is followed by a vowel-initial within the phrase, the two join into a single syllable (see Part VII, Section 3(C)).

Another point to remember is that colloquial English has "syllabic consonants," whereas Italian has none. In colloquial English, the consonants *l, m* and *n* may be syllabic—that is, in an unstressed syllable they may take the place of a vowel. For instance, in *little, chasm, heaven* no vowel sound is heard in the unstressed syllable and the *l, m* or *n* substitutes for it.

This English characteristic may account for the tendency of some vocalists to anticipate an Italian *l, m* or *n,* and even to sing a complete note on one of these consonants, forgetting that Italian has no syllabic consonants in speech or in singing.

Consequently, in Italian every syllable, note and beat must necessarily include at least one vowel and no pitch should be sung on a consonant alone. In the following example to sing *da-n-za* for *da-an-za* and *a-l mio* for *a-al mio* is wrong.

"Danza, danza, fanciulla gentile" by Durante

EXAMPLES

Practice so that every note contains a vowel:

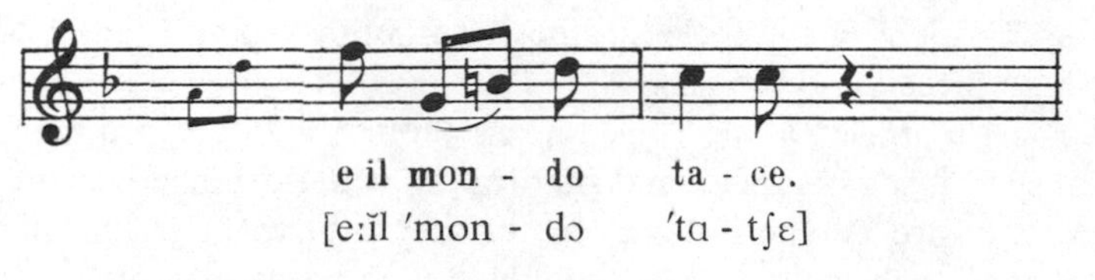

Le nozze di Figaro, Act IV

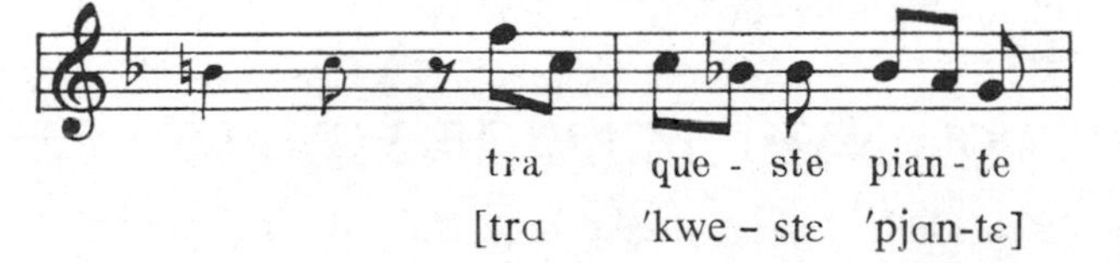

Le nozze di Figaro, Act IV

Tosca, Act II

La Bohème, Act I

Part VII

WORDS IN CONTEXT

INTRODUCTION

People who do not understand Italian sometimes interrupt a conversation and say: "Please go on speaking Italian and allow me to listen. It is such a lovely language. It sounds like music. It sounds like singing." One does not seem to hear the same remarks about other Western languages. What is the origin of the melodiousness, smoothness and fluidity of Italian which is so pleasing to the ear?

Some English-speaking singers even though they are using correct individual speech sounds speak and sing Italian with a foreign accent. What is it, then, they are missing? What should they add to their knowledge and skill to make their Italian sound genuine? The work that should be done, after acquiring correct speech sounds, to achieve perfect Italian diction will be discussed in this chapter.

1 THE DOMINANT ROLE OF VOWELS IN ITALIAN

One of the salient characteristics of Italian is the primary role played by the vowels.

Numerical Predominance Of Vowels

As with German, Danish, Swedish and other Germanic languages, English consonants and consonant clusters prevail over vowels. Words like *strength, flasks* and *plants* show that the backbone of English lies in its consonants.

On the contrary, the strength of Italian lies in its vowels. Like its sister languages in the Romance group, such as French, Spanish or Portuguese, Italian shows a marked prevalence of vowels, as in *eroe* [ɛ'ɾɔːɛ], *aereo* [ɑ'ɛɾɛɔ], *ideale* [idɛ'ɑlɛ].

If we compare the English verb *judge* with its Italian equivalent *giudicare* [dʒudi'kɑɾɛ] we will note that both stem from the Latin *iudicare*. But, whereas in English it developed into a monosyllable with a single short vowel, in Italian it remained quadrisyllabic with four vowels. Similarly the English monosyllable *join* is related to the Italian trisyllable *giungere* ['dʒundʒɛɾɛ] and *isle* to *isola* ['izɔlɑ]. Compared to English, the predominance of vowels in Italian is striking.

One factor that contributes to this prevalence of vowels is that in

Italian practically all words end in a vowel. Another is that the open syllables—those that end with a vowel—outnumber the closed ones—those that end with a consonant.

Furthermore, unlike colloquial English, there are no syllabic consonants in Italian (see Part VI on SYLLABIFICATION). Thus, every syllable contains at least one vowel, and in singing one proceeds from one strong vowel to the next. It is precisely this persistent continuity of vowels that builds the strong and long line of vocalization characteristic of a Bellini, Verdi or Puccini.

Basic Character Of Italian Vowels

A further characteristic of Italian is that it has front and back vowels only, which are basic vowels. Thus it lacks the English mid vowels, the French and German mixed vowels and the French nasal vowels. Perhaps one reason why Italian sounds so different from these other languages is that it has no neutral vowel [ə] (also called weak or schwa), which recurs so frequently in English, French and German, and confronts the singer with a special problem.

As a result of these factors, Italian displays an unbroken pattern of basic strong vowels, as unaffected by their position in word and phrase as by stress or lack of stress.

The Length Of Italian Vowels

In lyric diction, Italian vowels are long, except those that precede a doubled consonant. Therefore even a vowel preceding two or three different consonants should be sustained.

2 BASIC ASPECT OF THE ITALIAN CONTEXT

(A) The Boundaries Of Words

Traditionally, languages are viewed as a succession of words. Such an approach is pedagogically sound in dealing with vocabulary, grammar or syntax. But from a phonetic standpoint this concept is not always justified, since words are not necessarily aurally identifiable entities in spoken languages. In Italian, there is no difference in sound between *lamenta* [lɑ'mentɑ] (*he laments*) and *la menta* [lɑ'mentɑ] (*the mint*) or between *uno stile* [unɔ'stilɛ] (*a style*) and *un ostile* [unɔ'stilɛ] (*a hostile one*).

In some spoken languages the boundaries of words can be easily detected, in others not at all. More often than not, it is a matter of degree.

(B) Staccato Languages And The Glottal Stop

In German a "glottal stop" (also called glottal attack) is prefixed to all vowel-initials in words such as *Auge, einsam*. A glottal stop is a plosive consonant produced by the closure of the vocal cords and their subsequent sudden release through breath pressure. It is the throaty sound that is produced when coughing lightly. Its phonetic symbol is [ʔ]. This glottal stop, though not to be used in lyric diction, is a legitimate German speech sound used in conversation as well as on the legitimate stage.

In spoken German the glottal stop indicates the beginning of words starting with a vowel, and, at the same time, interrupts the continuity of exhalation and phonation. It is precisely these frequent interruptions which result in the characteristic German "staccato" pattern.

Unlike German, the glottal stop is not an accepted sound in English and should not be used. However, it is often heard in conversation ". . . in such a manner as to produce a harsh, tense, jerky sound in the throat." (*Good American Speech* by M. P. McLean, p. 135).

In English, according to such phoneticians as Bloomfield and Jones, the glottal attack appears before stressed vowel-initials in words and compound words (*awful, whenever*) and between vowels in words and phrases (*co-ordinate, go on*).

As with German, it indicates the boundaries of words and also causes interruptions in the flow of breath and speech. Thus, it may confer upon colloquial English a staccato character like that of German though not as marked and noticeable.

(C) The Italian Legato

Contrary to English, Italian, spoken as well as sung, lacks a glottal stop completely, and never separates words within the phrase. In this respect Italian resembles the other languages in the Romance group as much as it differs from the Germanic group.

A foreigner listening to Italian without understanding the language has no way of discerning where the words start and end, since they are all fused together.

Each phrase, uttered with the most perfect "legato," sounds like a single long flowing word. It is precisely this unrelenting, flowing smoothness, in addition to its predominantly vocalic pattern, that endows the language with its extraordinary, striking melodiousness. And it is just this aspect that may prove to be an obstacle to English-speaking singers. People tend to carry over into foreign languages the speech sounds of their mother tongue. Accordingly, English singers learning Italian will at first use the glottal stop without being aware of it (Stirling, *The Pronunciation of Spanish,* p. ix).

Learning to avoid the glottal stop and practicing a smooth legato will be an important aspect of a singer's training, not only for the sake of Italian diction but also for vocal technique. Thinking of attacking vowels away from the vocal cords and throat and high in the resonance chambers will save the vocal cords from much wear and tear.

Practicing The Italian Legato

EXERCISE I: Vowel-Initials

To achieve a smooth and even vowel attack, it may be helpful at the beginning to prefix the vowel with a very short *h*. This sound requires the vocal cords to be open and impedes the articulation of a glottal stop. Later, merely thinking of an *h* will be sufficient.

Speak, then sing:

ah ['ɑ]	esci ['ɛʃi]	addio [ɑd'diːɔ]
oh ['ɔ]	aita [ɑ'itɑ]	a terra [ɑt'tɛrrɑ]
eh ['ɛ]	infame [in'fɑmɛ]	udite [u'ditɛ]
ehi ['ɛːĭ]	orrore [ɔr'roɾɛ]	eureka [ɛːŭ'ɾɛkɑ]
ahimè [ɑːĭ'mɛ]	aprite [ɑ'pritɛ]	evviva [ɛv'vivɑ]
odi ['ɔdi]	alzati ['ɑltsɑti]	aiutate [ɑju'tɑtɛ]
entra ['entrɑ]	atroce [ɑ'trotʃɛ]	inneggiamo [innɛd'dʒɑmɔ]
urla ['urlɑ]	amami ['ɑmɑmi]	ammazzami [ɑm'mɑttsɑmi]

EXERCISE II: Vowels Consecutive within a Word

Speak, then sing, vowels that are consecutive within a word with a perfect legato. There should be no glottal stop as may be heard in conversational English in *co-ed, co-operate, re-enter,* which causes English-speaking singers to pronounce *Aida* [ɑ'ˀidɑ] instead of [ɑ'idɑ].

Sustain the first vowel until ready to start the second and connect it smoothly to the first.

paura [pɑ'uɾɑ]	maestro [mɑ'ɛstrɔ]	Aida [ɑ'idɑ]
viale [vi'ɑlɛ]	cruento [kru'ɛntɔ]	Sionne [si'ɔnnɛ]
beato [bɛ'ɑtɔ]	soave [sɔ'ɑvɛ]	Leonora [lɛɔ'nɔɾɑ]
viola [vi'ɔlɑ]	aita [ɑ'itɑ]	Traviata [trɑvi'ɑtɑ]
liuto [li'utɔ]	coorti [kɔ'ɔrti]	Abigaille [ɑbigɑ'illɛ]
teatro [tɛ'ɑtrɔ]	spiare [spi'ɑɾɛ]	Luisa [lu'izɑ]

EXERCISE III: Vowels Consecutive within the Phrase

Connect vowels contiguous in a phrase with a smooth legato. Sustain the vowel-final until ready to start the initial.

Some English and American publishers use a small ligature linking vowel-finals with vowel-initials to symbolize the required legato. No Italian publisher would do this, since an Italian would not know how to articulate a glottal stop and to separate words.

In the present exercise we will use this ligature.

tu ami [tu'ɑmi]	disfida ebbe [di'sfidɑ'ɛbbɛ]
cara alma [kɑɾɑ'ɑlmɑ]	è in stranio ['ɛ:ĭn'strɑnjɔ]
chi è [ki'ɛ]	nostri oppressor ['nɔstriɔpprɛs'sor]
chi entra [ki'entrɑ]	Ah! infame io son [ɑ:ĭn'fɑmɛ'i:ɔ'son]
è ora [ɛ'oɾɑ]	vendetta avrò [vɛn'dettɑ'vrɔ]
tre anni [tre'ɑnni]	Donna Anna [dɔn'nɑnnɑ]
poichè è [pɔ:ĭ'ke'ɛ]	novantanove anni [nɔvɑntɑ'nɔvɛ'ɑnni]

EXERCISE IV: The Apostrophe

In Italian spelling, an apostrophe is used when an unstressed final vowel is elided in front of the initial vowel of the following word, for example *l'idolo* ['lidɔlɔ] for *lo idolo,* and *un'aura* [u'nɑ:ŭɾɑ] for *una aura.*

In English elisions occur rarely and only in poetry (*th'immortal, th'eternal*), but in Italian they occur often, in common speech and poetry.

An apostrophe does not separate words; it unites them, since it symbolizes the joining in a single syllable of the consonant of one word with the following vowel-initial.

The frequency of the apostrophe in Italian is intimately connected with its legato style.

Speak, then sing, with a perfect legato:

dov'è [do'vɛ]	mal'assetto [mɑlɑs'sɛttɔ]
dov'era [do'vɛɾɑ]	dell'onor [dɛllɔ'nor]
anch'io [ɑŋ'ki:ɔ]	quell'invida [kwel'linvidɑ]
nell'ira [nɛl'liɾɑ]	sull'aria [sul'lɑɾjɑ]
dell'alma [dɛl'lɑlmɑ]	all'amor [ɑllɑ'mor]

3 PHONETIC CHANGES RESULTING FROM THE LEGATO

OUTLINE

As a result of the Italian legato, neighboring words smoothly blended within the phrase may so influence one another that they undergo phonetic changes in their initial or final sound.

These changes, which are peculiar to Italian, acquire added importance in lyric diction.

Within the phrase, the following four possibilities arise:

(A) two or more vowels may be contiguous
(B) two consonants may be contiguous
(C) a consonant-final may precede a vowel-initial
(D) a vowel-final may precede a consonant-initial

This is the order in which these phonetic changes will be discussed.

(A) Two Or More Vowels Contiguous In The Phrase Sharing One Note

OUTLINE

Two, three or even four vowels consecutive within the phrase and belonging to two or three different words may merge into a single syllable. Together they form a "phrasal diphthong," "triphthong" or "double diphthong" and are sung on a single note.

DISCUSSION

One of the more striking peculiarities of spoken and sung Italian, not shared by English, French or German, results directly from its characteristic legato. When a vowel-final is followed by a vowel-initial within the phrase, and when only one or neither bears the word's stress, these vowels act as the two elements of a diphthong and blend into a single syllable.

As with all diphthongs, one of the vowels will be syllabic and sustained. The other, the nonsyllabic, will be very short.

EXAMPLE

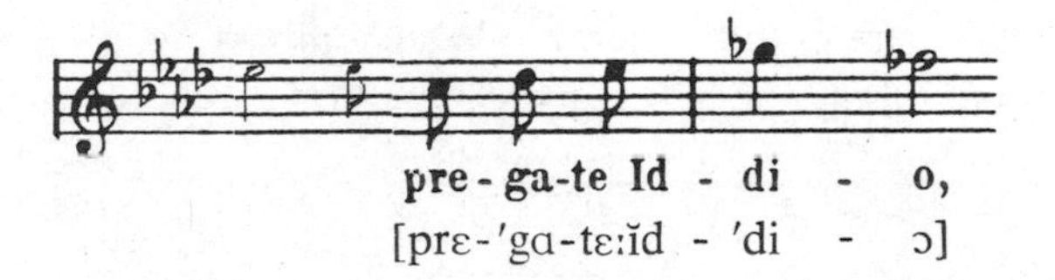

Cavalleria rusticana

Both words are trisyllables. However, since the final *e* and the initial *i* are both unstressed, they join syllabically to form, in this instance, a falling diphthong. The *e* is the syllabic and the *i* the nonsyllabic. Consequently, the sum of the two trisyllables will be not six syllables but five, so that the notes required will also be only five.

In the same fashion triphthongs and double diphthongs arise within the phrase.

This merging of two or more vowels of different words into a single syllable makes Italian vocal music often appear to have more vowels and individual syllables than notes to sing them on. But what appears to the eye does not necessarily correspond to aural reality. And one should fix firmly in one's mind that, in accordance with the principles of Italian, whatever letters share the same musical note in vocal music do so because they belong to the same syllable.

Thus, non-Italian singers who may have felt impelled to add notes and change a quarter-note into a duplet or triplet so as to have one note for each vowel were not familiar with the principles of Italian.

And it is unfortunate that some excellent musicians have failed in their editing of Italian Baroque music, in spite of their outstanding knowledge, for the simple reason that they have not followed the principles of the Italian language.

For Italian, which looks so simple to the eye, has phonetic patterns of its own, not the least of which is this peculiar merging of vowels.

HOW TO SING SEVERAL VOWELS SHARING ONE NOTE

In discussing diphthongs and triphthongs within the word, it was stated that there is invariably one among the vowels which is syllabic. The other, or others, are nonsyllabic.

This also occurs with diphthongs, triphthongs and double diphthongs within the phrase. One among the two, three or four vowels will be syllabic and will receive almost the entire length of the note value. The other or others will be extremely short, though certainly not weakened (see Part V).

The singer's first task will be to learn how to identify the vowel which is syllabic.

HOW TO IDENTIFY THE SYLLABIC

Although there is no general rule encompassing all possible vowel agglomerations within the phrase, most patterns adhere to the following three basic principles.

RULE I

Among several vowels sharing one note, a vowel stressed within a word takes precedence over unstressed ones and will be syllabic.

RULE II

If one of the vowels is an *i* or *u* unstressed within the word, it will be nonsyllabic, no matter whether it precedes or follows the other vowel.

RULE III

The vowel of an unstressed part of speech (an article, preposition or conjunctive pronoun) will be nonsyllabic, since by its very nature it is subservient to a stronger, stressed part of speech (noun or verb) whose vowel will be syllabic.

In the following pages, examples will be given to illustrate the patterns according to which vowels cluster within the phrase.

(1) Phrasal Diphthongs

When two vowels consecutive within the phrase join in a diphthong and share the same note, three possibilities arise:

a) a stressed final may be followed by an unstressed initial (. . . finchè avranno . . . [fiŋ'keːă'vrɑnnɔ], *La Gioconda,* Act I)

b) an unstressed final may be followed by a stressed initial (. . . Susanna ella stessa . . . [su'zɑn'năella], *Le nozze di Figaro,* Act I)

c) an unstressed final may be followed by an equally unstressed initial (. . . e tutta illanguidita . . . ['tuttɑːĭllɑŋgwi'ditɑ], *Pagliacci,* Act I)

The fourth possibility of a stressed final being followed by an equally stressed initial is of no concern here, since these two vowels can not share the same syllable, and will be set on two different notes. Just see to it that there is no break and glottal attack between the two stressed vowels.

EXAMPLE

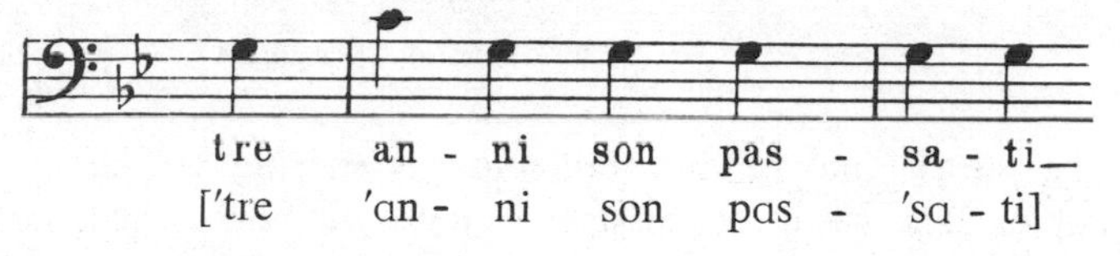

Madama Butterfly, Act II

The three possibilities listed above will now be discussed.

(a) STRESSED VOWEL-FINAL FOLLOWED BY UNSTRESSED INITIAL

The stressed final is syllabic and will receive almost the entire length of the note value. The nonsyllabic initial is very short though not weakened.

Speak, then sing:

EXAMPLE

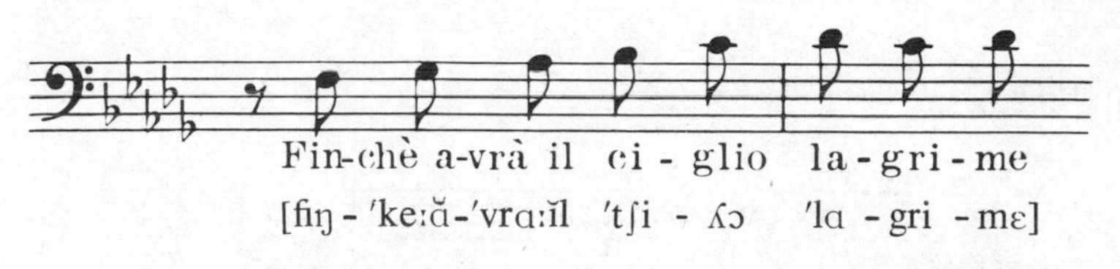

La Traviata, Act III

In the following example *un* is a monosyllable unstressed in the phrase. The stressed vowel-final is syllabic.

EXAMPLE

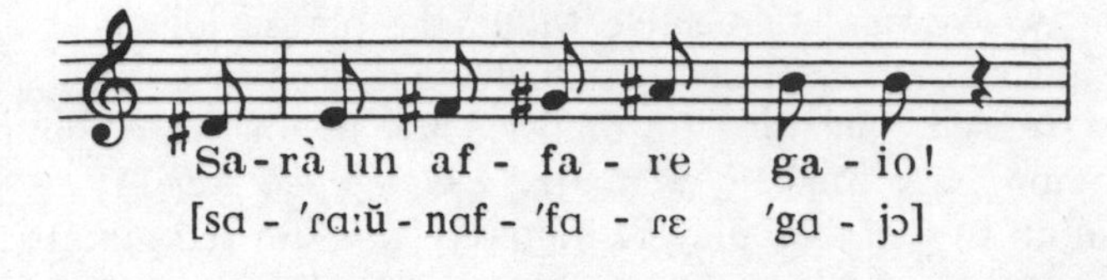

Falstaff, Act II

In the following example, a stressed and strong monosyllable precedes an unstressed vowel-initial. The vowel of the monosyllable is syllabic.

EXAMPLE

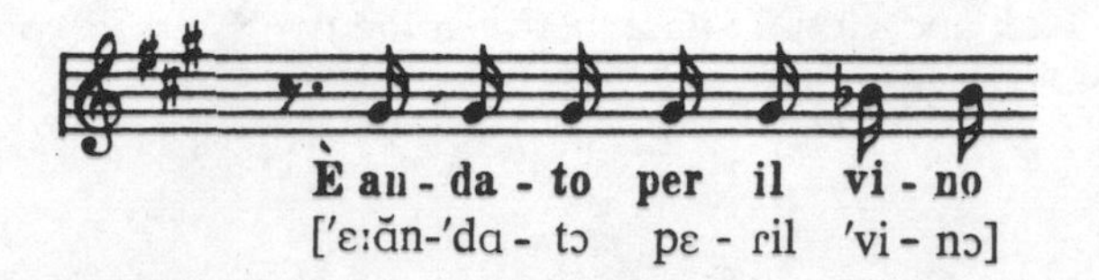

Cavalleria rusticana

In the phrase that follows, both vowels sharing one note belong to monosyllables. The vowel of the strong monosyllable *è* is syllabic.

EXAMPLE

La Traviata, Act II

In the last example, a stressed vowel-final is followed by an identical but unstressed initial. There should be no break and one single vowel sound should be heard.

EXAMPLE

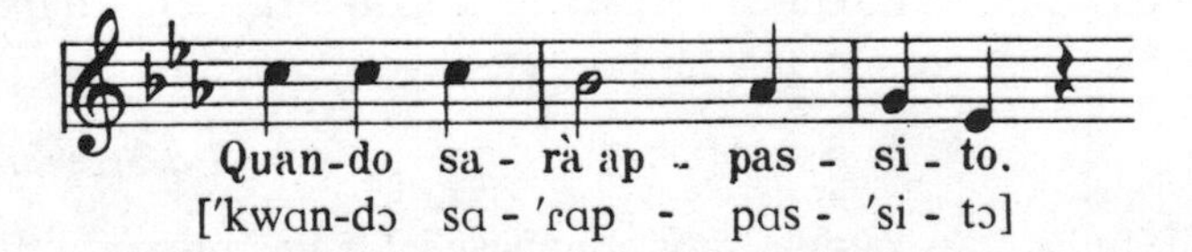

La Traviata, Act I

(b) UNSTRESSED VOWEL-FINAL FOLLOWED BY STRESSED INITIAL

The stressed vowel-initial is syllabic and long. The nonsyllabic final is very short though not weakened.

EXAMPLES

Le nozze di Figaro, Act III

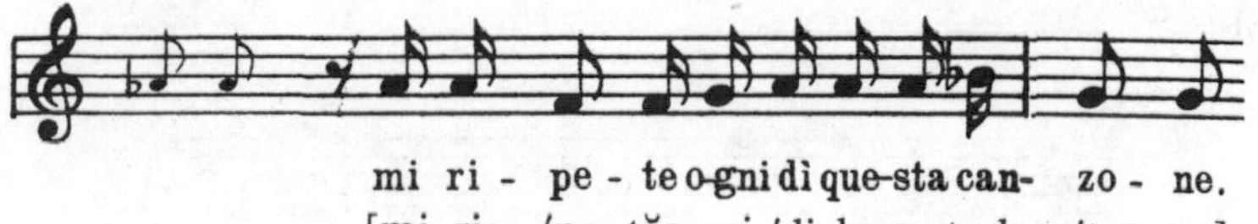

Le nozze di Figaro, Act I

When a final *e* [ɛ] or *o* [ɔ] is nonsyllabic, as in the last example, there is a general tendency to close it so that it ends up sounding like [j] or [w]. This is not permissible. Concentrate on opening it.

The next example illustrates an unstressed final preceding a monosyllable stressed in the phrase, as the verb *è*. The vowel of the monosyllable is syllabic.

EXAMPLE

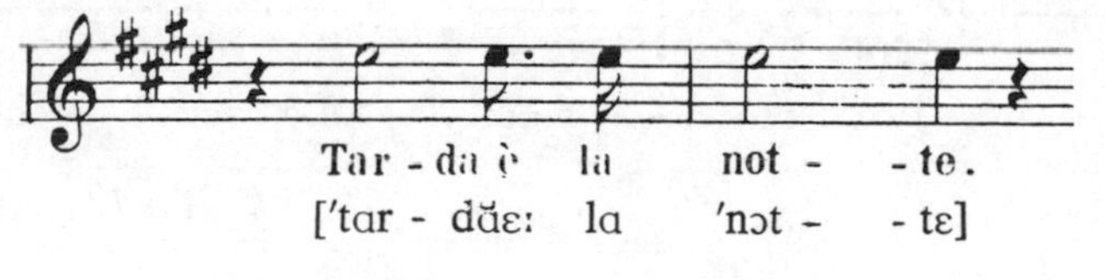

Otello, Act I

In the following example, both vowels sharing the same note belong to monosyllables, one stressed, the other unstressed in the clause. The vowel of the stressed monosyllable, the verb *han,* is syllabic.

EXAMPLE

La Bohème, Act I

The final *e* of *che* in the example above should be clearly open. It should not sound like a semiconsonant [j].

In the instance of an unstressed vowel-final followed by an identical stressed initial, as in the example that follows, there should be no break and one single vowel sound should be heard.

EXAMPLE

Pagliacci, Act I

In the next examples an unstressed open vowel-final is followed by the same letter but with a close sound. The open final is silent. Only the stressed close initial is sung.

EXAMPLES

La Traviata, Act II

Le nozze di Figaro, Act I

Le nozze di Figaro, Act I

The two preceding examples show that not even a punctuation mark separating two words can impede vowels from merging into a single syllable within the phrase. More examples of this kind will be given later.

This should be further proof of the strength of the Italian syllable as well as of the power with which the Italian legato overcomes obstacles.

(c) UNSTRESSED VOWEL-FINAL FOLLOWED BY UNSTRESSED INITIAL

If the unstressed final is either *i* or *u,* it will be nonsyllabic but not weakened. Rather, it should sound like [j] or [w].

EXAMPLE

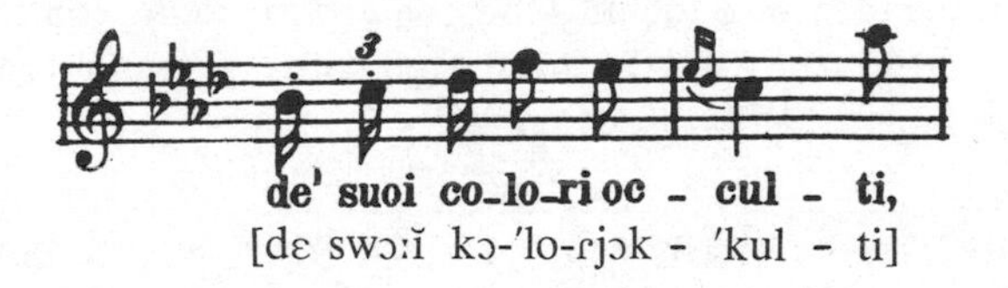

La Traviata, Act I

When the unstressed final is either *a, e* or *o,* in lyric diction this final will be syllabic and sustained.

EXAMPLES

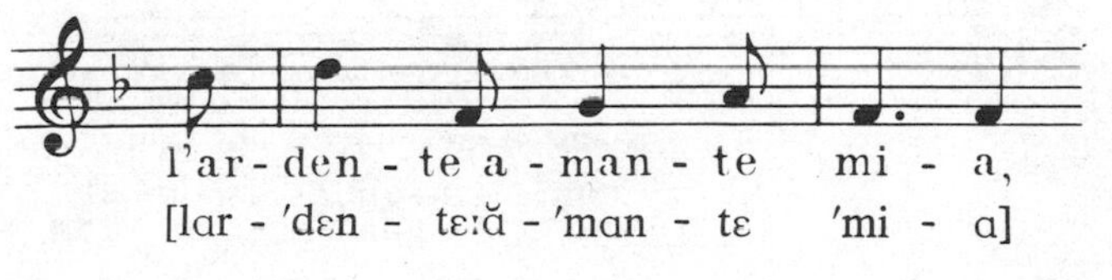

Tosca, Act I

[nɔn ˈpɔs-sɔːĕn - ˈtrɑr nɔ ˈnɔ]

La Bohème, Act III

If an unstressed vowel-final is followed by an identical unstressed initial, the two vowels will blend into one.

EXAMPLE

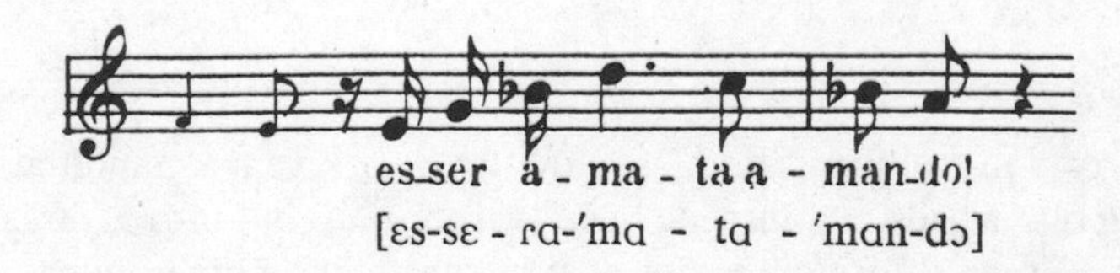

La Traviata, Act I

(2) Phrasal Triphthongs

Italian has triphthongs within the word, and, as a result of its legato, triphthongs within the phrase, too.

In conversation and poetry three consecutive vowels (or a semiconsonant and two vowels) belonging to two or three different words within one phrase often function as the elements of a triphthong and blend into a single syllable. In singing, these three vowels will share a single note.

A singer must learn to identify the one vowel among the three which is syllabic. To help him do so, the most frequently encountered patterns of phrasal triphthongs will be discussed.

(a) ONE OF THE THREE CONTIGUOUS VOWELS IS STRESSED WITHIN THE WORD

In this instance the stressed vowel will be the syllabic in the triphthong. It should be given almost the entire length of the note.

EXAMPLES

Le nozze di Figaro, Act IV

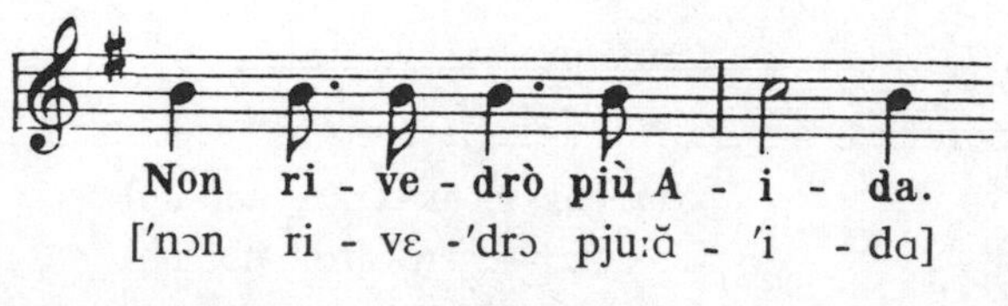

Aida, Act IV

(b) THE THREE CONTIGUOUS VOWELS INCLUDE THE MONOSYLLABLE *ho, hai, ha, è, e,* OR *o*

In such an instance the monosyllables *ho* [ˈɔ], *hai* [ˈɑːĭ], *ha* [ˈɑ], *è* [ˈɛ], *e* [ˈe] or *o* [ˈo] will be syllabic.

EXAMPLES

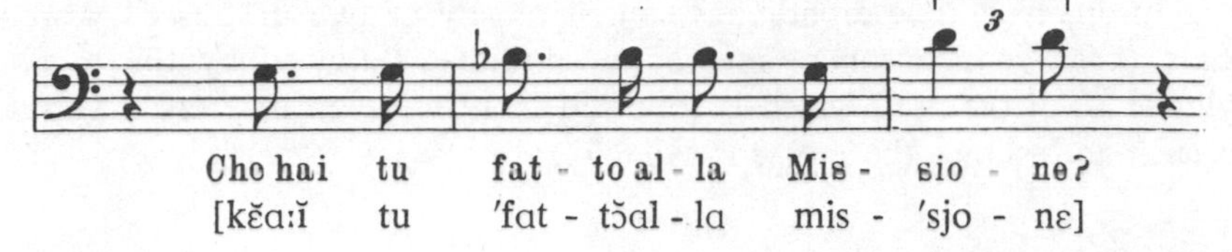

Madama Butterfly, Act I

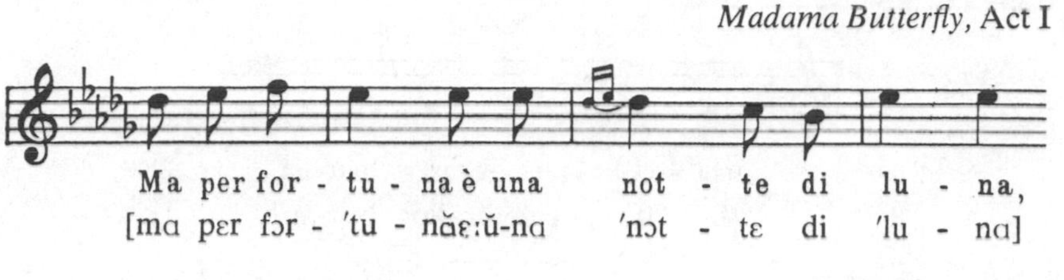

La Bohème, Act I

(c) NONE OF THE THREE CONTIGUOUS VOWELS IS STRESSED WITHIN THE WORD

In such an instance the second vowel is syllabic.

EXAMPLES

La Bohème, Act I

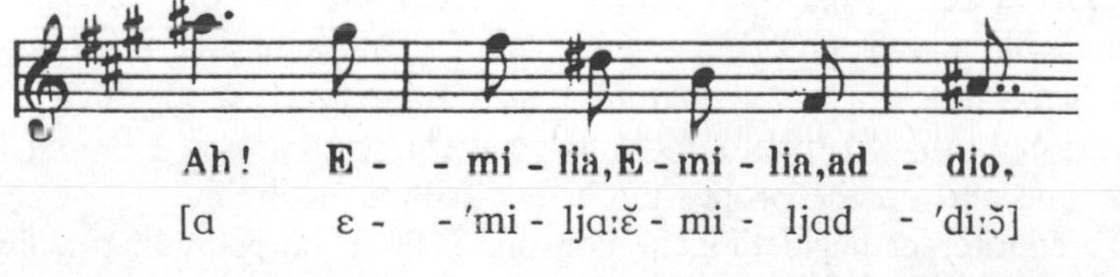

Otello, Act IV

(3) Phrasal Double Diphthongs

Double diphthongs are sequences of four vowels, or of one semiconsonant and three vowels, uttered in the same syllable.

There are no double diphthongs in English nor are there any in standard Italian within the word. But Italian has double diphthongs within the phrase, and singers must learn to identify the syllabic vowel. Almost the entire length of the note value should be assigned to it.

In opera, double diphthongs consist mostly of two unstressed vowel-finals (or a semiconsonant and a vowel-final), followed by the monosyllable *e* [ˈe] or *è* [ˈɛ] which is followed in turn by an unstressed vowel. In such an instance the *e* or *è* is syllabic.

EXAMPLES

[fiŋ - ke ˈlɑ-ɾjăɛːăŋ-kor ˈbru-nɑ]

Le nozze di Figaro, Act IV

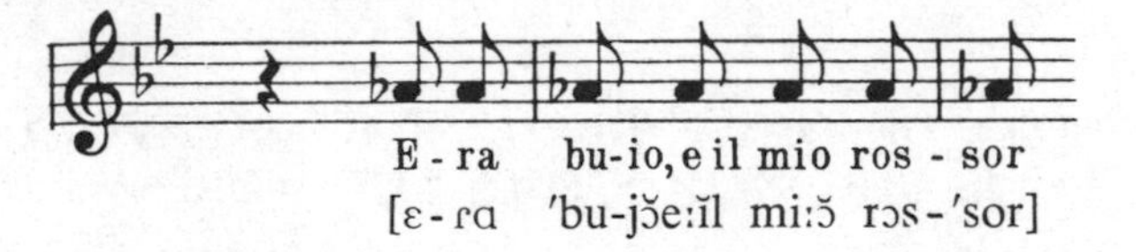

La Bohème, Act IV

(B) Two Consonants Contiguous In The Phrase

Two consonants contiguous in the phrase may be identical or different.

The consonants *l, m, n* and *r* are the only ones which may be final in Italian and are also the only ones which may be contiguous and identical within the phrase.

In the instance of *l* final being followed by *l* initial, or of *m* final by *m* initial, etc., singers tend to neglect, and even obliterate, the consonant-final. In *Le nozze di Figaro* the phrase ". . . *dal mio sen non trapassò* . . ." [dɑl miːɔ̆ˈsen nɔn trɑpɑsˈsɔ] sung by the Countess in her third-act aria, would then sound like ". . . *dal mio se non trapassò* . . . ," which is faulty diction. For both consonants have to be there, and should be sung at the proper time and on the proper pitch, but without a break.

To counteract neglecting the consonant-final, one should practice anticipating it and sustaining it beyond its required length.

Though the two identical consonants should not be separated, still they should sound like the two individual consonants they are, and not like a single prolonged one. To achieve this, the consonant-initial should be started with an audible breath impulse—that is, with an increased intensity of breath support marking the beginning of the new word. Such a breath impulse will have to be more intense than the one used for the articulation of a double consonant within the word.

Speak, then sing:

EXAMPLES

Otello, Act III

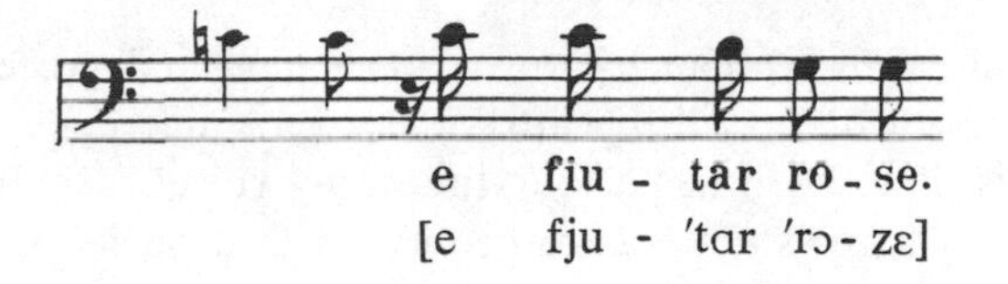

Don Giovanni, Act I

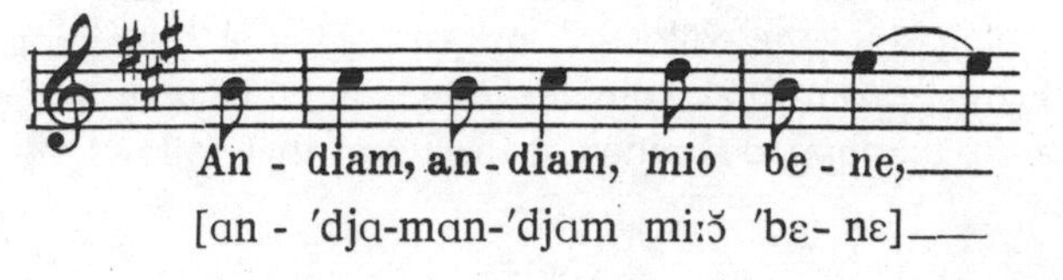

Don Giovanni, Act I

As to the second instance of two different consonants contiguous in the phrase, Part III stated that consonants adjoining in a word must be in perfect contact without any neutral vowel [ə] separating them. They must be in just as perfect contact when they follow each other in the phrase.

EXAMPLES

Un ballo in maschera, Act III

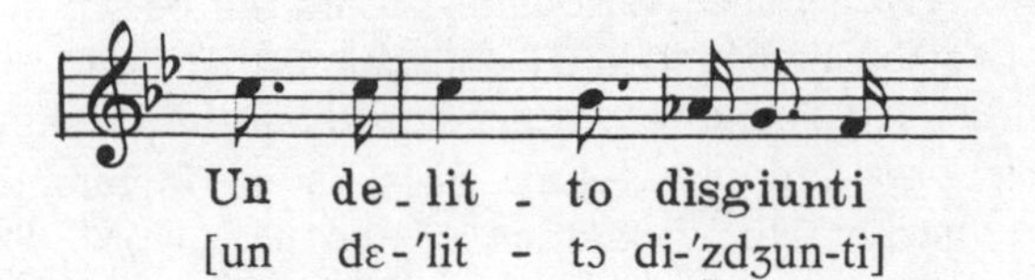

La forza del destino, Act IV

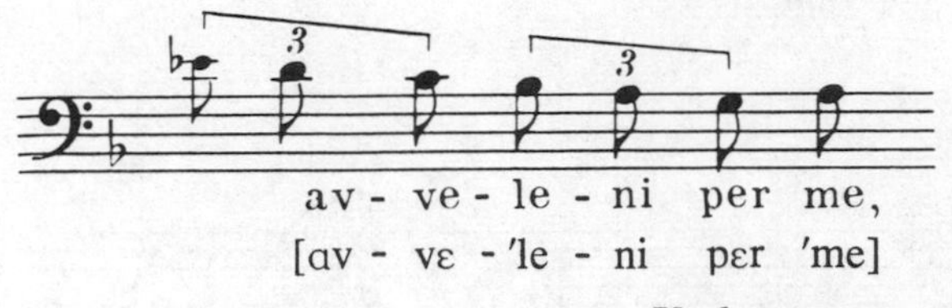

Un ballo in maschera, Act III

(C) A Consonant-Final Preceding A Vowel Within The Phrase

As a result of the Italian legato, a consonant-final preceding a vowel within the phrase acquires all the attributes of a single consonant between vowels. That is, it is short, has a long preceding vowel, belongs syllabically to the vowel that follows and has to be sung with it on its pitch and as the beginning of the next syllable and word.

Because of these attributes a final *r,* which is normally rolled, changes to a flipped *r* when followed by a vowel within the phrase.

Speak, then sing, the following phrases, greatly sustaining the vowel preceding the consonant-final, so as to utter that consonant as the short (in case of an *r,* as the flipped) initial of the word that follows.

EXAMPLES

Le nozze di Figaro, Act III

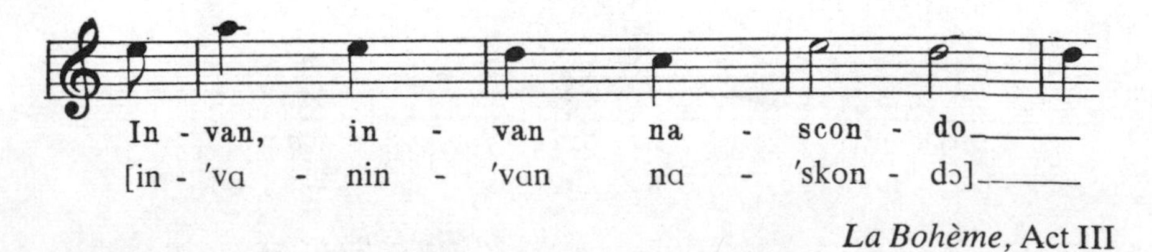

La Bohème, Act III

Madama Butterfly, Act III

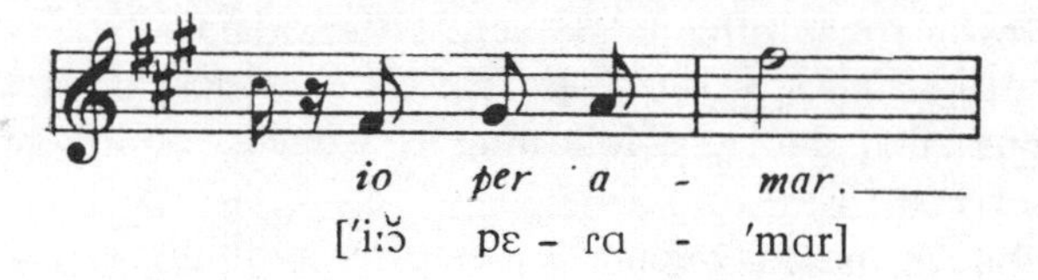

Otello, Act IV

(D) A Vowel-Final Preceding A Consonant Within The Phrase

The Phrasal Doubling

When a vowel-final precedes a consonant within the phrase, this consonant-initial may have to be doubled, under specific circumstances and rules. The vowel-final preceding such a consonant will have to be shortened, as when a vowel precedes a double consonant in the word.

Accordingly, the phrase "*A te, . . .*" (*Madama Butterfly,* Act II) should sound like [ɑt'te] and "*. . . perchè Signor, . . .*" (*Tosca,* Act II) like [pɛr'kessi'ɲor].

This "phrasal doubling" is another peculiarity of the Italian language. It is heard wherever good Italian is spoken. Moreover, in lyric diction it plays a special role, particularly in dramatic situations, in strengthening the delivery of words and text. It increases their chance of being heard and understood. This is vitally important when the voice is pitted against the acoustic impact of an orchestra and is why the phrasal doubling plays an important role in opera.

DISCUSSION

The initial consonant of a phrase should always be short. The doubling of a consonant-initial may occur only when it is medial in the phrase and is preceded by certain types of words. Here is the exact rule.

RULE FOR THE PHRASAL DOUBLING

A phrasal doubling occurs when a word starts either with a single consonant or with the consonants *bl, br, cl, cr, dr, fl, fr, gl, gr, pl, pr, tr* and when the word is preceded within the phrase by a strong monosyllable (see list below), by a polysyllable stressed on the final vowel or by one of the dissyllables listed below.

SPELLING

Normally the spelling does not show the phrasal doubling. It recognizes it only when the two words have merged in a single one, as in *lassù* [lɑs'su], a combination of *là* ['lɑ] and *su* ['su].

However, even this merging is not required and particularly in poetry and old scores one may often come across the original two words written separately, such as *là su*. Nevertheless, since the monosyllable *là* belongs to the strong ones that double a following consonant, orally such doubling must be observed.

Thus, though one may come across both spellings, *chissà* and *chi sa* [kis'sɑ], *sissignore* and *si, signore* [sissi'ɲoɾɛ], *frattanto* and *fra tanto* [frɑt'tɑntɔ], *giammai* and *già mai* [dʒɑm'mɑːĭ], orally the phrasal doubling must be there in either instances according to the rule.

LIST OF WORDS THAT CAUSE PHRASAL DOUBLING:

(a) THE FOLLOWING MONOSYLLABLES

a ['ɑ] prep.
ah! ['ɑ] interjection
che ['kɛ] pron., adj.
ché, chè ['ke] conjunction
chi ['ki] pron.
da ['dɑ] prep.
dà ['dɑ] v.
deh! ['dɛ] interjection
dì ['di] n.
dì ['di] v.
do ['dɔ] v.
e ['e] conjunction
è ['ɛ] v.
fa ['fɑ] v.
fé, fè ['fe] n.
fé ['fe] v.
fo ['fɔ] v.
fra ['frɑ] n.
fra ['frɑ] prep.
fu ['fu] v.
già ['dʒɑ] adv.
giù ['dʒu] adv.
ha ['ɑ] v.
ho ['ɔ] v.
là ['lɑ] adv.
lì ['li] adv.
ma ['mɑ] conjunction
me ['me] disjunctive pron.
né, nè ['ne] conjunction
no ['nɔ] adv.
o ['o] conjunction
o ['o] interjection (invocation)
oh! ['ɔ] interjection (exclamation)
più ['pju] adv.
può ['pwɔ] v.
qua ['kwɑ] adv.
qui ['kwi] adv.
re ['re] n.
sa ['sɑ] v.
se ['sɛ] conjunction
sé, sè ['se] disjunctive pron.
sì ['si] adv.
so ['sɔ] v.
sta ['stɑ] v.
sto ['stɔ] v.
su ['su] prep.
te ['te] disjunctive pron.
tra ['trɑ] prep.
tre ['tre] cardinal number
tu ['tu] pron.
va ['vɑ] v.
vo' ['vɔ] v.

REMARK

Not all monosyllables cause the doubling of a following consonant-initial. Only the strong monosyllables in the list above do so. Weak monosyllables, such as the articles *lo* ['lɔ], *i, gli* ['ʎi], *la, le* ['lɛ] or the conjunctive personal pronouns *lo* ['lɔ], *li, la, le* ['lɛ] do not.

EXAMPLES

Speak, then sing, the following phrases, energetically shortening the vowel preceding the phrasal doubling and lengthening the double consonant itself.

Cavalleria rusticana

Madama Butterfly, Act I

La Traviata, Act III

Tosca, Act II

La Bohème, Act III

REMARK

Several phrasal doublings in one phrase may be detrimental to the characteristic Italian vowel line and should be avoided. Which one (or ones) is chosen may be a matter of context and also of individual taste and artistry.

The only general advice that can be given is to avoid phrasal doublings consecutive in the phrase. Thus, though *e, tu* and *che* are all doubling monosyllables, the best way to sing the following phrase is:

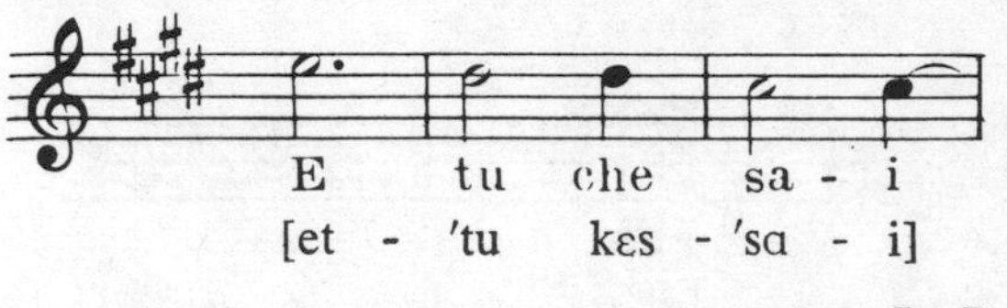

La Bohème, Act II

(b) ALL POLYSYLLABLES WITH ACCENTED VOWEL-FINAL

such as *perchè* [pɛr'ke], *così* [kɔ'zi].

EXAMPLES

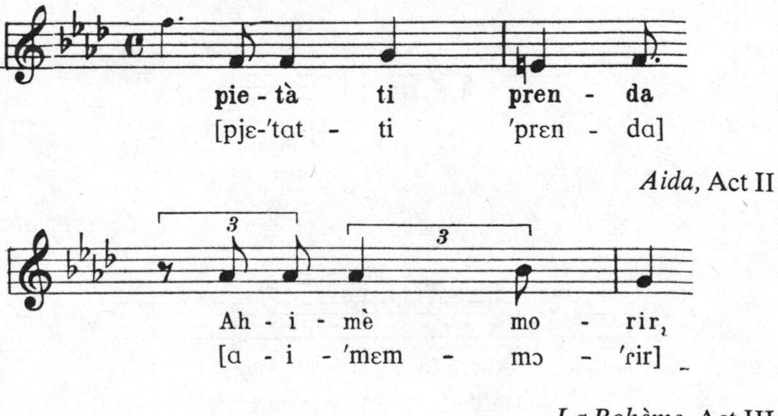

Aida, Act II

La Bohème, Act III

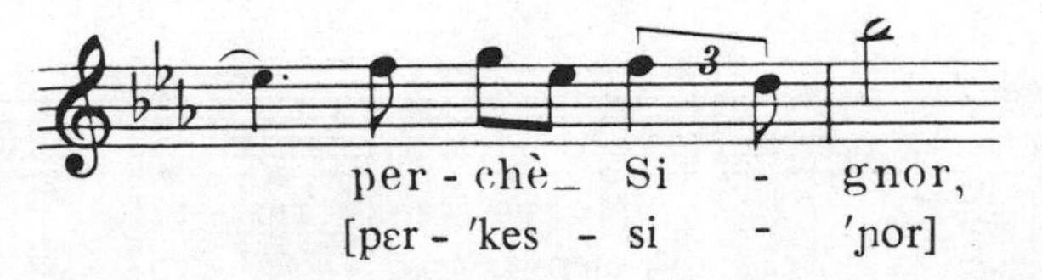

Tosca, Act II

(c) THE FOLLOWING DISSYLLABLES

come ['komɛ], *contra* ['kontrɑ], *dove* ['dovɛ], *ove* ['ovɛ], *qualche* ['kwɑlkɛ], *sopra* ['soprɑ], and *sovra* ['sovrɑ].

EXAMPLES

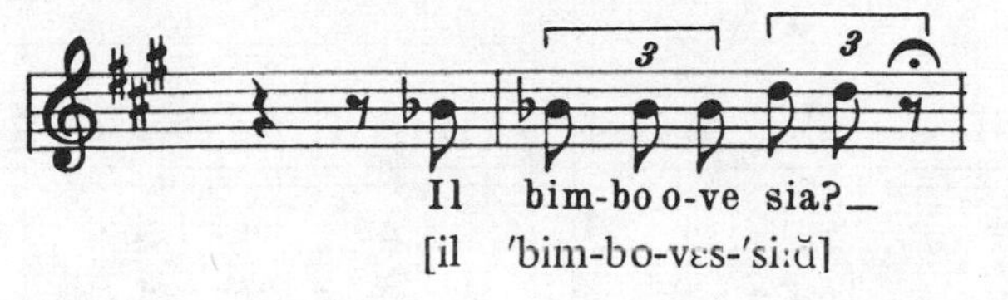

Madama Butterfly, Act III

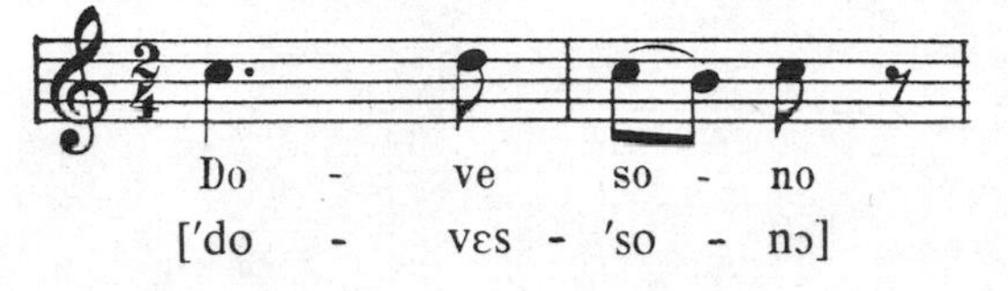

Le nozze di Figaro, Act III

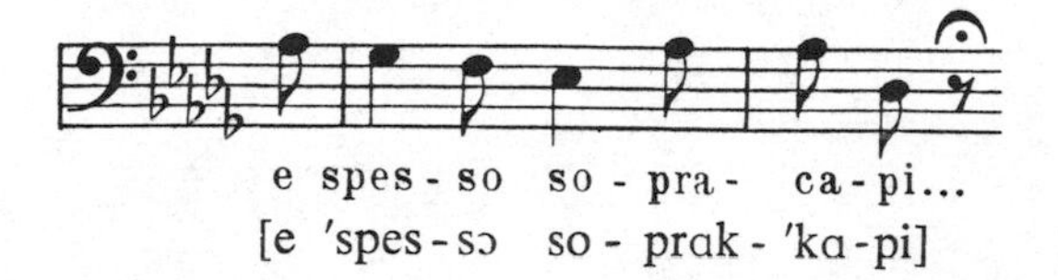

La Bohème, Act I

REMARK

THE WORDS *Dio, Dei, Dea, Dee,* AND *Maria*

The initial of *Dio* ['diːɔ̆], *Dei* ['dɛːĭ], *Dea* ['dɛːɑ̆], *Dee* ['dɛːɛ̆] and *Maria* [mɑ'riːɑ̆] (when the latter stands for the Virgin Mary) is always doubled, provided it is preceded by a vowel within the phrase.

EXAMPLES

Otello, Act IV

Madama Butterfly, Act I

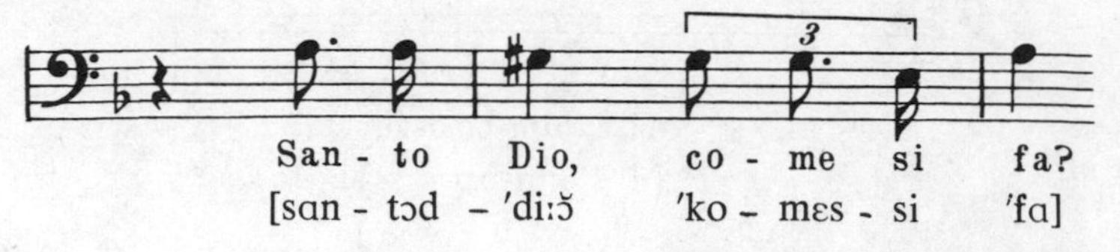

Madama Butterfly, Act II

Appendix I

UNSTRESSED *e* AND *o*

1) Many Italian text books state that unstressed (including unstressed final) *e* and *o* are close.

2) Others maintain just as unequivocally that they are open.

3) As to authoritative philologists and phoneticians, one states that unstressed *e* and *o* ". . . have sounds intermediate between the close and the open . . ."; [1] another that ". . . il existe des (voyelles) moyennes qu'on n'avait pas reconnues jusqu'ici."; [2] a third that their closing or opening depends on their position in word and syllable; [3] and a fourth that they ". . . si ravvicinano nelle sillabe semiforti e si confondono nelle sillabe deboli. . . ." [4]

4) The fact to consider is that text books, as well as phoneticians, discuss the timbre of unstressed *e* and *o* in Italian speech without taking into consideration the changes occurring in the transition from speech to singing.

5) According to Virgil Thomson: ". . . conversational speech and shouted speech do not observe the same vowel qualities. . . . But the great orators and the great actors, when working without a microphone, still project their phrases through vowel observances that at a lower level of loudness would be considered frank distortion. Singing requires even greater distortion of speech customs, since tonal resonance must be preserved at all times." [5]

6) It is because of this requirement that French lyric diction makes certain allowances (see May Laird-Brown, *Singers' French,* N. Y.: Dutton, 1926, pp. 87, 88, 89) as does German (see Eva Wilcke, *German Diction in Singing,* N. Y.: Dutton, 1930, p. 139), and English (see Madeleine Marshall, *The Singer's Manual of English Diction,* N. Y.: G. Schirmer, Inc., 1953, pp. 124, 163, 164, 168). So does Italian lyric diction.

7) Conversationally, Italian is spoken so rapidly that it is difficult to establish the timbre of these unstressed *e*'s and *o*'s, which may account for this diversity of opinion.

8) On the legitimate stage, well-trained actors who, speaking without

[1] C. H. Grandgent, *From Latin to Italian,* Cambridge: Harvard University Press, 1927, p. 35.

[2] F. M. Josselyn, *Études expérimentales de phonétique italienne,* Paris: Publications de la "Parole," 1901, p. 173.

[3] E. B. Davis, "Italian E's and O's," *Italica,* XIV, 4, 120.

[4] A. Camilli, *Pronuncia e grafia dell'italiano,* Florence: Sansoni, 1947, p. 34.

[5] Virgil Thomson, "Music and Musicians, Singing English," New York Herald Tribune, April 12, 1953.

a microphone, have to slow down so as to project their lines show a distinct tendency toward opening these unstressed vowels.

9) Singers, who in addition have to deal with their increased voice range and abnormally extended vowels, face an added problem. Some of them have tried to solve it by opening indiscriminately all *e*'s and *o*'s, stressed as well as unstressed.[6] But this is unacceptable, since it changes the vowel pattern of the language, and often the meaning of words as well.

10) But the opening of the unstressed *e*'s and *o*'s only, including the finals, is practiced by many prominent singers, and sounds most convincing. It does not distort the pattern of the language, inasmuch as a stressed open vowel, because of its stress, will sound a shade more open than the corresponding unstressed one which gives the text its proper sound balance.

11) It is correct to open unstressed *e* and *o* in lyric diction, but not to over open them (see p. 22).

[6] Luigi Biagioni, *Italienische Lautlehre für Musikstudierende und Musikfreunde*, Cologne: P. J. Tonger, 1929, p. 5.

Appendix II

INTERVOCALIC *s*

All Italians do not pronounce the intervocalic *s* in the same manner. Northern Italians voice it and Southern Italians unvoice it. In Tuscany, a region in Central Italy, the two trends meet. Here the intervocalic *s* is sometimes voiced and sometimes unvoiced; there is no recognizable pattern. Also there are variations not only from one Tuscan city to another, but even from one city district to the next.

Linguistically, each one of these trends is justifiable and consequently acceptable. Since the voicing or unvoicing of intervocalic *s* does not identify different words, we share the opinion of those who consider it normal to pronounce it either always voiced, or always unvoiced. (A. Camilli, *Pronuncia e grafia dell'italiano,* and B. Migliorini, *Pronunzia fiorentina o pronunzia romana?* See Bibliography.)

Since the voiced *s* has greater carrying power, it is best for a singer to voice intervocalic *s,* which is what is usually done on the lyric stage.

Appendix III

THE SEMICONSONANT [j]

The rule in Part IV, Section 6 states that in Italian lyric diction the letter *i* may be considered a semiconsonant whenever, in a polysyllable, it shares one note with a following vowel.

In Italian speech the case is not quite as simple, since not only a semiconsonant [j], but also a short unstressed, and therefore nonsyllabic, vowel [i] may share a syllable with a long following syllabic vowel. Thus the *i* in the final syllable of the words *odio* ['ɔdĭɔ], *celia* ['tʃɛlĭɑ], *patria* ['pɑtrĭɑ], *solitario* [sɔli'tɑɾĭɔ] and the *i* in *violenza* [vĭɔ'lɛntsɑ], *sapiente* [sɑ'pĭɛntɛ] are not semiconsonants. They are short nonsyllabic first front vowels [i].

But inasmuch as the difference between a [j] and an unweakened short unstressed [i] is not too noticeable, and inasmuch as English-speaking singers tend to weaken unstressed vowel sounds, the simplified rule as formulated in paragraph one above is helpful toward sounding an unstressed short [i] as strong and as unweakened as it should be.

The scientifically inclined reader who wants to know exactly when, and when only, an *i* stands for a semiconsonant may find the exact rules in A. Camilli's *Pronuncia e grafia dell'italiano.* They are given here in a somewhat abridged form.

An *i* is pronounced [j]:

1) when initial followed by a vowel: *ieri* ['jɛɾi]

2) when between two syllabic vowels: *gaia* ['gɑjɑ]

3) in the noun and adjective endings *-iero* ['jɛɾɔ], *-iere* ['jɛɾɛ]: *cameriere* [kɑmɛ'ɾjɛɾɛ] (*arciere* [ɑr'tʃɛɾɛ], however, has a silent *i*)

4) in the verb endings *-iamo* ['jɑmɔ], *-iate* ['jɑtɛ]: *cantiamo* [kɑn'tjɑmɔ] (but with verbs whose stems end with *c, g, sc, gl, gn,* the *i* is silent)

5) when the *i* derives from a Latin short open *e* or from Latin *ae* or from a Latin *l: dieci* ['djɛtʃi], *lieto* ['ljɛtɔ], *fiamma* ['fjɑmmɑ] (but notice that *cielo* ['tʃɛlɔ] and *cieco* ['tʃɛkɔ] have a silent *i*).

Appendix IV

DICTIONARIES

Since there is no Italian dictionary using the IPA, those dictionaries that symbolize the opening or closing of Rule III *e*'s and *o*'s by other means are recommended. Some dictionaries use acute and grave accents, others use dots, italicized print, etc. See, for example, the Edgren, Garzanti, Hoare and Reynolds dictionaries listed in the Bibliography.

Not acceptable to a singer are those dictionaries that try to convey the pronunciation of Italian *e*'s and *o*'s by means of conventional English spelling. They would use the spelling *ay* for an open as well as for a close *e* without distinguishing. Actually an English *ay* stands for the diphthong [eĭ] which has nothing to do with Italian pronunciation.

BIBLIOGRAPHY

Baglioni, Silvestro. *Udito e voce*. Rome: Tumminelli, 1924.

Bertoni, Giulio, and Francesco A. Ugolini. *Prontuario di pronunzia e di ortografia*. E.I.A.R., 1939.

Biagioni, Luigi. *Italienische Lautlehre für Musikstudierende und Musikfreunde*. Cologne: Tonger, 1929.

Bloomfield, Leonard. *Language*. New York: Henry Holt & Co., 1933.

Bodmer, Frederick. *The Loom of Language*. New York: Norton & Co., 1944.

Borrometi, Giovanni. *Grammatica italiana della lingua viva*. Palermo: Andò, 1945.

Busnelli, Manlio D., and U. Pittola. *Guida per l'insegnamento pratico della Fonetica Italiana*. Perugia: Regia Università Italiana per stranieri, 1940.

Camilli, Amerindo. *Pronuncia e grafia dell'italiano*. Florence: Sansoni, 1947.

———. *An Italian Phonetic Reader*. London: University of London Press, 1921.

——— and Daniel Jones. *Fondamenti di grafia fonetica*. London: International Phonetic Association, University College, 1933.

Castiglione, Pierina Borrani. *Italian Phonetics, Diction and Intonation*. New York: S. F. Vanni, 1957.

Colorni, Evelina. "The Basis for Bel Canto." *Opera News,* March 28, 1955.

———. *Lessons in Italian Lyric Diction*. New York, 1956.

Conti, Iginio. *Fisiopsicopatologia del linguaggio*. Milan: Bocca, 1952.

Davis, Edwin B. "Italian E's and O's." *Italica,* XIV, No. 4, December 1937.

Della Corte, Andrea. *Canto e bel canto*. Turin: Paravia, 1933.

Edgren, Hjalmar. *An Italian and English Dictionary*. New York: Henry Holt & Co., 1944.

Ellis, Alexander J. *Pronunciation for Singers*. London: J. Curwen, 1877.

Enria, Umberto. *Prontuario ortofonico-ortografico*. Milan: Il Maglio, 1960.

Fanfani, Pietro. *Vocabolario dell'uso toscano*. Florence: Barbèra, 1863.

Garzanti. *Garzanti Comprehensive Italian-English, English-Italian Dictionary*. New York: McGraw-Hill, 1962.

Genévrier, Pierre. *Précis de phonétique comparée*. Paris: Didier, 1927.

Georges-Calonghi. *Dizionario della lingua latina*. Turin: Rosenberg & Sellier, 1951.

Grandgent, Charles Hall. *From Latin to Italian*. Cambridge: Harvard University Press, 1927.

Gröber, Gustav. *Grundriss der Romanischen Philologie*. Strassburg: K. J. Trübner, 1888/1902. Revised 1933.

Hall, Robert A. *Descriptive Italian Grammar*. Ithaca: Cornell University Press, 1952.
Hecker, Oscar. *Il piccolo Italiano*. Freiburg: Bielefelds, 1921.
Heffner, R. M. S. *General Phonetics*. Madison: University of Wisconsin Press, 1949.
Hoare, Alfred A. *A Short Italian Dictionary*. Cambridge: University Press, 1954.
Jones, Daniel. *An Outline of English Phonetics*. New York: Dutton, 1956.
———. *The Pronunciation of English*. Cambridge: University Press, 1956.
———. *An English Pronouncing Dictionary*. London: J. M. Dent & Sons, 1948.
Kenyon, John S., and Thomas A. Knott. *A Pronouncing Dictionary of American English*. Springfield, Mass.: G. and C. Merriam Co., 1953.
Lamperti, Francesco. *Guida teorico pratica elementare per lo studio del canto*. Milan, 1864.
———. *L'arte del canto*. Milan: Ricordi, 1883.
Malagoli, Giuseppe. *Ortoepia e ortografia italiana moderna*. Milan: Hoepli, 1912.
———. *L'accentazione italiana*. Florence: Sansoni, 1945.
Mancini, Giovanni Battista. *Pensieri e riflessioni pratiche sopra il canto figurato*. Vienna, 1774.
Marshall, Madeleine. *The Singer's Manual of English Diction*. New York: G. Schirmer, Inc., 1953.
McLean, Margaret Prendergast. *Good American Speech*. New York: Dutton, 1947.
Meyer-Luebcke, Wilhelm. *Grammatica storica della lingua italiana e dei dialetti toscani*. Turin: Chiantore, n. d.
Migliorini, Bruno. *Pronunzia fiorentina o pronunzia romana?* Florence: Sansoni, 1945.
———. *Linguistica*. Florence: Le Monnier, 1950.
———. *Consigli per una buona pronuncia italiana*. Turin: Fonit-Cetra, n. d.
Ovidio, Francesco D'. *Dieresi e sineresi nella poesia italiana*. Milan: Hoepli, 1910.
Panconcelli-Calzia, Giulio. *Italiano; fonetica, morfologia, testi*. Leipzig: Tuebner, 1911.
Passy, Paul. *Petite phonétique comparée*. Leipzig and Berlin: Tuebner, 1922.
Pestelli, Leo. *Parlare italiano*. Milan: Longanesi, 1958.
Reynolds, Barbara. *The Cambridge Italian Dictionary*. Cambridge: University Press, 1962.
Rousselot, Jean. *Principes de phonétique expérimentale*. Paris: Didier, 1924.
Setti, Dora. *Fonetica e dizione*. Milan: Vallardi, 1958.
Stirling, William F. *The Pronunciation of Spanish*. Cambridge: University Press, 1935.

Tosi, Pietro Francesco. *Observations on the Florid Song*. London: Wilcox, 1743.

Trabalza, Ciro, and Ettore Allodoli. *La grammatica degl'Italiani*. Florence: Le Monnier, 1934.

Wilcke, Eva. *German Diction in Singing*. New York: Dutton, 1930.

Zingarelli, Nicola. *Vocabolario della lingua italiana*. Bologna: Zanichelli, 1959.

INDEX